THE INF[illegible]NCE
With A Heart Method

How To Position Yourself As An Expert, Authority, or Thought Leader by Writing Your Book

So You Can Do More Good For
More People With Your Business

BEN GIOIA

The Influence With A Heart Method
How To Position Yourself As An Expert, Authority, or Thought Leader by Writing Your Book
So You Can Do More Good For More People With Your Business

ISBN: 978-1-64184-434-5

Legal and Earnings Disclaimer:
While all attempts have been made to verify information provided in these materials and its ancillary materials, neither the author or publisher assumes any responsibility for errors, inaccuracies, or omissions, and is not responsible for any financial loss by the customer in any manner. Any slights of people or organizations are unintentional. If advice concerning legal or related matters is needed, the services of a qualified professional should be sought. The information contained in these materials is strictly for educational purposes. Therefore, if you wish to apply ideas contained in these materials, you are taking full responsibility for your actions. Neither the author nor publisher purport these materials as a "get rich scheme" and there is no guarantee, express or implied, that you will earn any money using the strategies, concepts, techniques, and ideas in these materials. Earning potential is entirely dependent on the efforts and skills of the person applying all or part of the strategies, concepts, techniques, and ideas contained in these course materials. Any examples, stories, or case studies are for illustrative purposes only and should not be interpreted as examples of what consumers can generally expect from these materials. No representations in any part of these materials are promises for actual performance. Any statements and strategies offered in these materials are simply opinion or experience, and thus should not be misinterpreted as promises, results, or guarantees (express or implied).

This material and its associated ancillary materials are not intended for use as a source of professional financial, accounting, legal, personal, or medical advice. You should be aware of the various laws governing business transactions or other business practices in your particular geographical location. The author and publisher disclaim any warranties (express or implied), merchantability, or fitness for any particular purpose. The author and publisher (Ben Gioia, Influence With A Heart® or any of Ben Gioia's representatives) shall in no way, event, or under any circumstances be held liable to any party (or any third party) for any direct, indirect, punitive, special, incidental, or other consequential damages arising directly or indirectly from any use of this material, which is provided "as is," and without warranties. PRINTED IN THE UNITED STATES OF AMERICA

What People Are Saying About Ben Gioia and His Strategies

"At 9:00 p.m. last night, my book hit #1. Thank you for your supreme guidance and expertise in starting this book."

—CRISTINA DIGIACOMO, M.S.
Industrial Philosopher™, Author: *Wise Up! At Work*,
C-Suite Network Advisor

"Ben Gioia is changing business for the better through what he teaches. I truly believe that his insights about influential communication and leadership will support those people—who have ideas and strategies proven to help transform the world—to brand and package what they offer for distribution on a larger scale."

—K.L.K, PhD, Mark T. Greenberg Professor
for the Study of Children's Health and Development
Assistant Professor in the Department(s) of
Nutritional Sciences and Food Science
Pennsylvania State University

"He already helped me write one. Now, he's going to help me with another. Why? Because Ben is the best book coach."

—WHITNEY VOSBURGH
Author of *Work The Future! Today* and *Brand New Purpose*, Speaker, Interim Fortune 20 CMO

"What resonates the most with me about Ben is his heartfelt and patient approach, blended with skillful coaching aimed at achieving results. Ben offers an array of ideas, resources, and a strategic plan that gives traction to your vision while staying connected to the heart of your business."

—ANNETTE SEGAL
CEO and Founder, The Valiant Group
Executive and Leadership Coaching

"My book will be out soon, and in addition to being a dream come true that it's done, it's also, finally, a book that shares who I am with the world! Thank you, Ben!"

—ANNEMARIE SHROUDER (SHE, HER)
Helping People Thrive Int'l Speaker | Consultant, Facilitator: Diversity, Inclusion & Belonging | Racial Equity, Member: Evolutionary Business Council

"I am delighted to be writing the book that's just been WAITING to be written. I trust Ben to be the support I need, along with accountability PLUS his clear understanding of my mission—and he is seriously good at what he does. It was a no-brainer to say YES!"

—CHRISTINE POWERS
Founder and CEO at Philosophers Camp, keeper of wonder & wisdom, empowering voices to uplift

"I wouldn't have written my book without Ben's help. His unique ability to quickly create clarity, along with his insights, turned the complicated task of writing a book into a simple one: By the end of the first coaching call, I was no longer staring at a blank page!"

—JESSE ALI
Founder at LimitlessAbs.com

"Thank you to Ben for the exceptional guidance and service you are giving our cohort as part of your Write Your Book in 5 Weeks course. We are all having daily epiphanies, and it is helping us write the best books we can!"

—MIRIAM (MIZ) FEILER
Build yourself. Build your networks. Build your business.

"Ben is an incredibly talented coach. His partnership has helped me to quickly deliver several critical elements of my brand and positioning that I had been challenged to accurately produce on my own. I highly recommend Ben—if you're an organization, entrepreneur, or change agent who's looking for a heart-based collaborative partner to represent, elevate, and best express your authentic message... with power, heart, and profound clarity."

—STEVE HAVILL, CEO, Change Agent
Conscious Business Consultant
Certified High Performance Coach

"Ben Gioia's brilliant system and masterful tutelage make the step-by-step process of writing a book and using it as a powerful marketing tool seem simple. I highly recommend him as a master coach and guide for writing and positioning your book to take your business to the next level!"

—JAMES WOEBER
Co-Founder and Director at Art of Heartful Living

"Ben, thanks again for all your help in getting my book published! It went live today and your insight was invaluable. Your input and edits were a great boon and really helped me in the way I approached telling the story.

—RALPH MILLER
Author of *Christ Lives in You*

"It's very hard to find something that really impresses me like what Ben Gioia is teaching. I'm so glad he's sharing this simple method to guide people to writing their books the right way!"

—GIUSEPPE FRATONI
Strategic Marketing for Attorneys, Consultants, and Professionals Who Want To Grow A Sustainable Practice

"I was tasked by a Fortune 100 company to find a consultant on the topic of empathy and customer experience. While my search yielded tens of candidates, I was fortunate enough to find Ben."

—FARZAD WAFAPOOR
Apps, VR, and 360 Video for
Business, Education, and More

"Ben is an artist when it comes to honing a message to the essence. I have worked with Ben to help me with my new positioning in the technology space.

"With a long list of achievements, and not exactly a straightforward story, he had quite the challenge on hand. I loved his process; he was the facilitator weaving all the bits together in a truly amazing way."

—BARBARA WITTMAN
Creator: The Trusted CIO Advisor Blueprint™
Trusted CIO&IT Advisor • Author • SAP Retail Consultant

"Ben offered a wise, listening ear when I was faced with an unexpected opportunity to transform my personal brand. Inspired by Ben's coaching, I found the position I love!"

—C.G., Communications Strategist
Global Tech & Communications for Salesforce.com

"Man, the growth was insane during that time! Over two hundred followers, 25 discovery calls, and 70 real leads. The messaging was a game-changer."

—"COACH CHRIS" HINES, Podcaster
Greatness Unlimited

From the offices of
Leadership Awake, LLC
San Francisco, CA, USA

Hey, it's Ben,

People often ask me, "How do I position myself as an expert (or authority or thought leader)?"

"Keep it simple and keep smiling," I answer.

★ BY DEVELOPING a clear message, unique offer, and proven method, in a book that connects your "special sauce" to what your clients want and are looking for...

★... AS YOU KEEP WALKING the path that you're guiding others along, grounded in your experience, hard-earned wisdom, case studies, stories, and successes...

★... SO YOU CAN CREATE more connections, referrals, and value by aligning your positioning, messaging, and one-of-a-kind offer!

Simply put, write your book as soon as possible.

I know you can write a profitable, high-quality book, fast.

(I did it in five weeks, and it transformed my business.)

Now, imagine your business and your life with your book done!

Find out the details so you can get your book DONE at 5WeekBook.com. I look forward to connecting with you!

Cheers,

Ben

Ben's First Book, The #1 Best Seller

"This is a must-read for any salesperson, business owner, or entrepreneur. *Marketing With A Heart: How To Use Trust Based Marketing For Greater Income, Influence, and Impact* is not just about marketing and selling; it is about communicating with people. Ben shares his incredible heartfelt experiences and principles to help build lasting relationships in any business. I am recommending this book to all of my clients."

—JOHN FORMICA
An "Ex-Disney Guy," Speaker, and Author
America's Customer Experience Coach

Nearly 40 case studies provide real examples of Ben's teachings and how they can be most effectively applied to different businesses, organizations, and movements. Get it here (print or digital): amazon.com/author/bengioia

"Coaches, consultants, teachers, and leaders with a message of service—read this book and join me in following Ben's lead. Together we can elevate and enlighten the practice of reaching out and offering our gifts and talents to those whom we are meant to serve."

—LOU D'ALO, Founder of PowerUpCoaching.com
Marketing for Enlightened Business Owners

Did You Know?

Your ability to make an even bigger impact in the world happens when you:

1) Express your unique purpose

2) Communicate with empathy

3) Tell your story while maximizing and leveraging your thought leadership, positioning, and influence

MARKETING WITH A HEART will help you do this—whether you're an executive, entrepreneur, small business owner, speaker, leader, author, coach, consultant, solopreneur, or visionary. You will become a better communicator and a more influential leader.

This #1 best seller is available in print for all of your favorite devices and is ready for purchase worldwide.

###

"No matter the industry—for any of us to make a bigger impact—we need to present ourselves bigger, brighter, and bolder than ever before. We need to pump up the volume: how we present and use our authority, thought leadership, and influence. Let's do it in a way that creates connection and trust while building lasting relationships!"

—Ben Gioia

For you — for being more and more of you — and bringing your love, light, and truth into the world!

Foreword

I've spent my life (and my entire career) studying the lives of people who started movements that changed the world.

How did transformational leaders like Gandhi, Dr. King, Jesus, Mother Teresa, and the Buddha do what they did? I became obsessed with that question.

Acting on advice from one of my earliest mentors, I made it my mission to understand, not only how they did it, but why they were successful when so many others were not.

The results led me to develop an entire framework that helps people replicate the same types of results in their chosen fields.

The results are also why I love Ben Gioia so much.

The main takeaway from my extensive body of work is that there isn't simply a "what" to do. There is also a "how" that it is absolutely crucial in achieving the outcome that matches your "why".

Let me explain.

If you take two professional basketball players and ask them how they make a free throw, dunk the ball, play defense, or run a triangle offense, they will both explain the "what" with impeccable precision. They know "what to do" to win the game.

But what makes a player like Michael Jordan stand out so far above the crowd? It isn't just that he knows the game, the right strategy, and the way to properly involve his team.

It's his profound way of embodying what drives those behaviours, plus a certain ontology (way of being) that is uniquely his. And that ontology isn't simply a choice; it's a hard-earned life lesson.

It's something that's revealed, only from digging deep inside, and finding something that other people aren't (yet) willing to take the journey... to discover.

And that's precisely what Ben Gioia has to offer.

Ben paid the price to write this book because he has lived it. This is a labor of love, an expression of his soul's desire to serve: by passing along the timeless wisdom he's earned and by allowing that wisdom to transform his life first hand.

In the early years of sharing my Movement Maker Blueprint (based on the work of Gandhi and Dr. King), I had a profound realization. As I taught the mechanics of how to turn a message into a movement, I saw companies consuming the content and applying it to their marketing campaigns (and bottom lines) with tremendous success.

But I started to notice that hardly anyone asked, "If you've reverse-engineered how to create movements, like those of Gandhi and Dr. King, why aren't there more Gandhis or Dr. Kings?"

Good question. And I'm happy to say that things are changing now, and that's why Ben's book is right on time.

People want to make a difference. They aren't satisfied punching a time clock and collecting a paycheck. People want to do something meaningful, and they want their work to be an expression of their deepest held principles.

Ben Gioia is one of those people.

If you're reading this book, you're probably one of them, too. And there's a chance that you might be asking yourself, How can I do what Gandhi or Dr. King, or Mother Teresa have done?

Ben walked away from lucrative (but unsatisfying) careers to find a path that aligned with his heart. He set out on a journey of self-discovery to get clarity on what was most important to him. He's been courageous enough to look within and see how his own adversities contribute to his hard-earned life lessons, and his heart is called to figure out how to help others to do the same.

Ben exercised the discipline required to master some of the things many of us only aspire to and allowed himself to become the change he wants to see in the world.

When Ben teaches his clients to write their bestselling book, for example, he does so from a place of authority: outwardly (because he's mastered the techniques and strategies), and inwardly (because the things he speaks, writes, and teaches are authentic and genuine).

What you'll discover in these pages has the power not only to help you change your business, but to transform you personally. It can purify your heart, make you kinder and more patient, and instill in you a deeper sense of loving-kindness and purpose.

And isn't that what you really want?

Not just to achieve more, but to become a more full expression of your true nature? That's why you picked up this book.

There are many people who can teach you how to do marketing, how to position yourself within your niche, how to write a book, or many of the other aspects of the "what" of influence that Ben teaches.

Yet, he stands alone.

Ben teaches how to do all this in a way that is authentically you and aligns with the principles of compassion, loving-kindness, and empathy. So your tools of influence will have a profound impact—not just on your bank account—but on the world at large.

I have experienced Ben's work firsthand. I have seen how his students change their view of the books they are writing: from a powerful positioning piece to an authentic expression of their soul's deepest desire to serve.

At the same time, I am a witness to Ben's personal journey of integrating his spiritual ideals with his business. He has created this book as a guide (and so much more) so you can do that for yourself.

"Integrate the spiritual with the secular." That advice came from my early mentor and set me on this path to helping people start movements. Applying the principles in Ben's book will help you maximize that same advice.

During my lifelong journey of studying the lives of people who changed the world for the better, this integration is exactly "how" you unlock your innate capacity to do the highest good that you came into the world to do.

Thank you, Ben Gioia. Not only for writing this book, but for living in such a way that you embody these principles for all of us to model.

—Joseph Ranseth
Speaker, Author, Transformationist
Founder of the Movement Maker Method™
JosephRanseth.com

Table of Contents

What People Are Saying About Ben Gioia
and His Strategies iii
Ben's First Book, The #1 Best Seller x

Foreword 1
Why This Book Is Right On Time 12
Taking Your Stand and Making a Bigger Impact 13
How to Use This Book and What to Expect 16

Your Mission: To Inspire More People to Say
YES—to Your Ideas, Vision, Message,
Product, or Service—Again and AGAIN! 18
The Influence With A Heart® Method 21
Debunking The 7 Worst Myths About Writing Your
Book (So You Can Make It Happen) 22
A Quick Hello 24
Being Clear on Your Purpose
Increases Your Power to Influence 27
An Innovative Approach: Principles vs. Values 29
An Open Invitation For Us To Chat 35
The Framework: Influence With A Heart® 37
This Is How And Why It Works 38
Ben's Story 42
Still Wondering How I Almost Died Four Times? 47

Chapter 1: START WITH SELF-CARE: Loving Kindness, Meditation, Forgiveness, and Letting Go 49

Summary: START WITH SELF-CARE 50

Meditation Is Not New, and People Are Finally Catching On To The Goodness It Offers 51

How to Quit Suffering Now (a.k.a. The Buddha Smile, My Signature Talk) 53

Forgiveness Meditation Instructions (Brief) 60

Drinking Coffee and Being Mindful About It 61

Creating Success by Telling Yourself a Story 66

One Success Habit Made Famous, Thanks to One Historical American President 71

Learning How to Keep Letting Go So You Can Be Happier and Make the Impact You Want 76

Chapter 2: EMPATHY 79

Summary: EMPATHY 80

Influence Is About Shaping the Future, So Connect the Dots and Make Your Vision Clear 81

Using the Psychology of Influence (Ethically) 83

How Well Do You Know Who You're Talking To? 84

Elevating Your Elevator Pitch 89

[What Are Your Thoughts or Insights?] 92

Case Study: Your Book Will Change Your Life 93

ACTION: Use More Empathy in All of Your Communication with These 5 Simple Steps 94

Chapter 3: STORY 97

Summary: STORY 98

The Power of Story in Leadership 99

Your Story Is Your "Special Sauce" 103

Logic (Alone) Never Changed the World 107

Mandela (and the Story Continues) 110

[What Are Your Thoughts or Insights?] 112

Case Study: It's Never Too Late for Your Book 113

ACTION: Choose 13 of Your Best Stories by Using These 7 Guidelines 114

Chapter 4: THOUGHT LEADERSHIP **117**

Summary: THOUGHT LEADERSHIP 118

Thought Leadership Is Influence In Action and a Key Component of Your Story 119

How to Stand Out Authentically and Uniquely 123

One of the Biggest Mistakes Thought Leaders Make When Communicating 128

7 Reasons Why the Buddha Was (and Still Is) an Influential Thought Leader 133

[What Are Your Thoughts or Insights?] 135

Case Study: Pivoting, Positioning, and Profiting 136

ACTION: Are You a Thought Leader? (Make Sure People Know These 7 Things About You) 137

Do You Want to Publish, Position, and Profit from Your Book? 138

Wrapping It All Up 140

Acknowledgements 145

THOUGHT
LEADERSHIP

Influence
WITH A HEART®

EMPATHY

STORY

Why This Book Is Right On Time

This is an amazing time in history. Consultants, coaches, solopreneurs, and speakers are moving humanity forward and enhancing life for more people. Organizations, leaders, and visionaries are creating amazing businesses, movements, and positive social change.

Why is this happening? Because more and more people are realizing that everyone and everything on this planet is interconnected. The impact these people are making is both worldwide and one-to-one.

- Now, imagine if each one of these people had more power to inspire more people to say yes!

- Imagine if each one of these people could quickly and easily make their influence exponential. This means they can cultivate more relationships, achieve more results, be more successful, and set a positive example in the world!

- Now, imagine what happens when all of these people—"turn up the volume" by writing a high-quality book so they can reach more people and impact more lives!

- Just imagine what's possible... (and I want to welcome you to the party)!

Taking Your Stand and Making a Bigger Impact

If you're like me, you want to make a bigger impact in the world. And if you think about it, making a bigger impact comes down to one key thing: using more influence in every aspect of your communication and leadership.

When you use more influence—and do it ethically—you inspire more people to take action that's good for them and good for you (win-win). This means more success for you, your organization or business, and those you serve.

Writing a book is a great way to make this happen. When you do this, it's easier for your audience, customers, collaborators, and clients to:

1. Find you and connect with you
2. Sign up for your list
3. Follow you and share on social media
4. Purchase your products
5. Invest in your services
6. Bring you more word-of-mouth referrals

7. Give you the opportunity to lead them or help them so they can create more influence and impact with their business, in their workplace, or in their life

Creating more influence by writing your book is a simple, effective way to use your business or organization for making real, positive change happen today and to lay the foundation for your unfolding legacy in the future.

Having a book is a powerful way to unify and clarify your positioning and messaging, especially:

1. For face-to-face conversations, on the phone, recording a video, creating a product, running a meeting, or speaking to an audience

2. During your speech, webinar, or training—so you can inspire more people, give them a new perspective, and show them powerful and positive next steps on the road to their success

3. In how you communicate—so you can move yourself, your team, or your organization into action

4. On your website—so the right people will be engaged, read your content, and join your list

5. Inside your emails—so people will open, read, and click to take action

6. In your LinkedIn summary—so the opportunities you want will come your way

7. During your discovery call or on your sales page—so you can rocket your influence, get more clients or customers, and make a bigger impact

In a nutshell, writing your book (whether it's your first or next one) is powerful and will help bring more clients and opportunities—even before you publish!

Why?

Because your book gets your clients, customers, colleagues, and audience inspired and excited about who you are and what you offer, so they can take action.

No matter what, people must understand that you are authentic, that you understand them, and that you care. (That's why they're going to choose you over the 100s if not 1,000s of other choices out there.

Your book helps inspire people to take action that's good for them, good for you, and good for everyone in the mix.

How to Use This Book and What to Expect

What you'll find in the following pages can be applied to multiple aspects of your business, your life, and your book. You will communicate more effectively, be a better leader, and make a bigger impact in the world.

You're about to discover concepts, perspectives, and strategies about influence and communication that you can use, model, and share with others right away.

The methods are presented in a clear, simple, and direct way, so you'll have no doubt about how and when to use your new insights, wisdom, and strategies.

This isn't like any other book you've read.

- It's saturated with takeaways (that can be applied by every person in every field and industry)
- It's based on proven methods and timeless principles that have been used by masters, orators, writers, innovators, experts, visionaries, and leaders throughout history and will continue into the future
- Although it's nonfiction, I've written this book as an unconventional narrative that's conversational and filled with stories, imagery, anecdotes, provocative

questions, action steps, humor, case studies, and multiple opportunities for you to reflect, learn, and take action

What I'm offering in this book is a framework for being a better communicator and a more influential leader (whether you're writing a book or not).

My intention is that you take what you learn (plus the wisdom you cultivate and the insights you experience) and create the influence, income, and impact you want.

You're about to discover a better way to do business and practical steps that you can take to make it happen. I wish you every possible success, and more!

Now, I invite you to take a few moments to be present so you can get the most out of what's inside. Shut the door, put your phone on "airplane mode," and get comfy.

Take a few deep, nourishing breaths, and smile.

Have a notebook handy, get some sticky notes, scribble in the margins, dictate your thoughts into your phone, and capture your discoveries...

As I tell you a little story about Influence With A Heart.

Your Mission: To Inspire More People to Say YES—to Your Ideas, Vision, Message, Product, or Service—Again and AGAIN!

Take a look at history and take a look at what's happening in our world right now. Influence is powerful (and sometimes scary) stuff.

In the wrong hands and used the wrong way, influence can be dangerous to your health, happiness, safety, spirituality, dignity, legacy, and freedom.

But in the right hands (like yours), just imagine what can happen when influence is used the right way! With more influence, you're able to inspire more people to take action. More people will say yes to you.

And remember: this is your one, single mission—no matter what. This is the one thing that absolutely must happen for you to succeed.

Your entire vision, mission, and message hinge on this.

You must inspire more people to keep saying yes!

(Otherwise, you won't have the influence and impact you want.)

This is how people get to know, like, and trust you. They understand that you're an expert, authority, thought leader, or influencer who connects the dots from what they want and need—to who you are and what you offer.

Thanks to your book, there are lots of powerful, valuable ways that people can (and will) say yes to you.

10 of the "big ones" are:

1. Choosing to visit your website, subscribing to your list, and opening your emails

2. Clicking on your call-to-action, joining your webinar, and investing in your coaching, training, or product

3. Connecting with you on LinkedIn or contacting you for an interview

4. Hiring you for a leadership position or consultancy

5. Inviting you to speak or train (onstage or online)

6. Offering you a partnership or an appointment

7. Investing in your services or events

8. Doing your marketing for you by telling their colleagues, clients, and community all about you

9. Signing up for your mastermind or leadership program

10. Actually 'doing the work' that will help them achieve the transformation they're looking for!

QUESTION: Which of those 10 "big ones" apply to you?

No matter who you are and what you do, these 10 "big ones"—these 10 yeses—are so important because they will help move your business forward fast.

It all starts by using more empathy, story, and thought leadership, whether you're face-to-face, online, onstage, or on the phone.

You'll automatically increase your influence, every time you communicate. You'll inspire and invite more people to say yes to making a choice that's good for them and good for you, whether it's opening your email, joining your presentation, or joining your team.

Whether you're an entrepreneur, visionary, or leader, just imagine how many lives you can impact with your ideas, message, vision, product, or service!

The Influence With A Heart® Method

(more) Loving-Kindness +
(more) Empathy +
(more) Story +
(more) Thought Leadership +
= Influence With A Heart®

- Loving-kindness happens when you relax your head, relax your face, smile, and feel the love in your heart.

- Empathy gives you the opportunity to see the world through another person's eyes. It creates connection and is the foundation for relationships based on trust.

- Stories create inspiration and an emotional experience for your reader or listener because they reach people's hearts as well as their minds.

- Thought leadership is your "secret sauce." (More on this later.)

You can use this framework anytime, anywhere, with anyone: in person, online, onstage, on the phone, in a training, in a video, during a speech, or in a meeting.

And especially when writing your book.

Debunking The 7 Worst Myths About Writing Your Book (So You Can Make It Happen)

Myth 1: "Writing a book is hard."

REALITY No it's not, as long as you have a plan and a clear understanding of what you'll include. And smile.

Myth 2: "I'm too busy."

REALITY You only have to write for a little more than one hour a day if you follow the right method.

Myth 3: "It's not worth my time."

REALITY If you put your book in the hands of 100 people, and 10% of them invested in your high-ticket program, how much would that be worth to you?

Myth 4: "You can't make money before it's published."

REALITY Actually, if you call yourself the "Forthcoming author of X," doing that can help you get in front of new, potential clients before you're even in print.

Myth 5: "The best books are chock full of facts and information."

REALITY The best books help people shift their ideas and beliefs (instead of just burying them with too much information). They make your reader want to contact you.

Myth 6: "You need to sell at least 20,000 books to make 6 figures or more."

REALITY You don't need to sell any! Because when you get your book into the hands of your ideal client, you can make an extra six figures from just one person saying yes to you. (Or two. Or 10. You get the picture.)

Myth 7: "Traditional publishing is better."

REALITY If you're a consultant, coach, solopreneur, or coach, self-publishing is better—over 94% of the time!

Because you get more control, more money, and more freedom to create the book you want on your terms.

(And you can be published in three months rather than the one or two years that often happens with traditional publishing! What do you think about that?)

A Quick Hello

Hi! I'm Ben Gioia ("joya"). I'm a three-time, best-selling author, and I make it easy for people to write a high-quality, #1 best selling book in just 5 weeks. (After that, it's publish and position right so you can profit fast.)

Thanks to 35+ years of print and digital publishing, I created The Influence With A Heart® Method. It's the best way for most consultants, coaches, solopreneurs, and speakers to publish their book—and position themselves for a media explosion—in just three months.

In years past, I helped a Fortune 100 company shift culture by creating an empathy video game (with MIT) for over 20,000 global employees. I also trained leaders at Stanford University and launched the world's biggest magazine (AARP).

I believe that all people are meant for great things.

And we thrive when we're peaceful and fully expressed. These days, I'm blessed to say that my teachings are used by more than 37,000 people around the world.

Once—while trekking in India (and facing death four times)—I received a gift: a fire inside to serve. Today, I help people inspire, influence, and impact the world. When you catch me on the stage—or virtually, around the globe—you'll discover my teaching: How To Quit Suffering Now (which I like to call The Buddha Smile).

In a former life, I had the privilege of improving the quality of life for people with ALS (e.g., Stephen Hawking, Lou Gehrig).

For me, loving-kindness and service are the names of the game:

★ I've been on retreats for 119+ days of silent meditation

★ I made friends with Death from three years of volunteering at hospice

★ I taught English to Tibetan refugees in India

★ The ALS Association gave me an award for creating a meditation program for people with ALS as well as the people who care for them

★ 10% of my monthly revenue (not profit) goes to people and organizations who make a difference

Some of my favorite clients and engagements include AARP, a Fortune 100 company, The ALS Association, Condé Nast, Hearst, MIT, Philosopher's Camp, Speakers

Who Dare, Stanford University, and USANA. (There are too many of my 5-week book writers to mention here!)

I also have a powerful story to share. During a hike in India, I almost died. 4 times in 72 hours!

Those 72 hours gave me profound gratitude for life and a fire inside to a create massive, positive impact.

First, I created and launched Marketing With A Heart™. Then I created and launched Influence With A Heart®.

I'm grateful to help people speak, write their books, and present themselves (and their business)—in a way that inspires positive action in the world around them.

I'm delighted that you're here right now and reading these words. May they support your happiness, success, and your ability to make a bigger impact!

In this book, you'll discover the same tools, techniques, strategies, and perspectives that I used to make my successes happen.

If you're ready to chat, I invite you to a no-sales, no hassles clarity call at InfluenceWithAHeart.com/connect so we can say, Ahoy!"

Being Clear on Your Purpose Increases Your Power to Influence

Your power and ability to influence—in a bigger way—start by being crystal clear on your purpose. This is true for individuals and it's true for companies, organizations, and movements.

When you know your purpose, these four things happen:

1. Work can be more inspiring, fun, and fulfilling (since it's an expression of who you are and why you're here)

2. You get more of the right things done faster and with less stress (since you're committed to your dream and can accept the fact that there will be hiccups, detours, and roadblocks on the way to achieving it)

3. You increase your ability to transform people's lives, because you're able to create a much more powerful connection and resonance with others)

4. You communicate and lead more effectively

Similarly, if you're part of a company, organization, or movement, purpose is just as important because it provides meaning and a connection to the bigger picture (mission and vision). As a result, these four things happen:

1. You (as well as your employees, colleagues, or team) are likely to be more productive, engaged, motivated, and happy

2. There is better communication, better team spirit, and increased job satisfaction

3. There is a greater understanding among different kinds of people which makes it easier to navigate conflict (because you're all working with a shared vision)

4. It helps create a culture of trust and engagement while inspiring innovation

Getting clear on your purpose is a foundation of success. But it doesn't stop there. Purpose needs to become part of the fabric of your business, organization, or movement. Like most things that are valuable in this world, it's a matter of making it happen and making it sustainable, so you stay focused and on the right path.

So how can you do this? Rather than using values to create alignment in your business, company, organization, or movement, I invite you to focus on the underlying principles instead.

An Innovative Approach: Principles vs. Values

I learned something very important from Steven Covey, author of *The 7 Habits of Highly Effective People*, which changed my business. Principles are not the same as values. Here's why:

- Values change according to time, place, situations, and the people involved. ("A woman's place is in the home" is a powerful example. Thankfully, we've come a long way, and there's still more work to be done.)

- Values create your beliefs: how you see the world, relate to others, interpret your experiences, and how you choose to act. (And sometimes you may not even understand why you do what you do.)

- Some of your values and beliefs may not be supporting your success because values and beliefs come (unchosen) from multiple people, places, and situations outside of ourselves.

- Values and beliefs affect everything in your life, leadership, outcomes, communication, marketing, selling, relationships, experiences, and success.

Think of it like this. Since values are guaranteed to change, how can you run your business (or your life) based on them?

Realistically, it's not going to work in the long run. So, I invite you to focus on principles instead.

Because principles are like gravity. They're a constant, expressing the core, unchanging elements of your purpose. They're like the North Star in your business or organization, keeping you (and everyone else) on track.

Covey's teachings (plus my own reflections and experience) inspired me to create and integrate my own 7 Principles of Influence With A Heart®.

These 7 Principles guide the choices and decisions (big ones and little ones) in my business and in my life. They help me express my purpose by offering me inspiration, clarity, and a roadmap. Here's how they look:

1. Principle of High-Integrity Success

I measure success through the people I serve, how I am living and expressing my purpose (in my life and business), and the influence I create.

- Since negative thoughts, words, and actions yield negative results, I do my best to focus on the positive/realistic, even in the most challenging circumstances.

- Sometimes this requires changing my habits, beliefs, perspectives, and attitudes because they affect others, my business, and me.

2. Principle of The Other Person's Shoes

All of my choices are informed by more than just my own perspective. When I am about to make a choice, I remind myself to ask these questions.

- How will this choice affect my client?
- What about other people that my business touches?
- And the community and the environment?
- How about the people who are alive seven generations from right now?
- Will everyone (and the Earth) benefit based on this choice? (Even wise choices sometimes have consequences.)

3. Principle of Truth and Respect

What I think, say, and do affects me and the people around me. Because of this, I do my best to be aware of my thoughts words, and actions.

- Do I feel open, calm, and spacious—or constricted, reactive, and defensive?
- Am I telling the truth (to others and to myself)?
- Am I treating people with respect?
- Am I relaxing my head, relaxing my face, and smiling?
- What is my tone of voice? How's my posture?
- How can I help elevate the situation through what I'm thinking, saying, or doing?

4. Principle of Growing and Sharing Abundance

I'm in business to make a difference and create abundance.

The more money I make, the more people I can influence and empower to do good their own good.

- I know money is a result of my service and the value I bring to others, not the goal unto itself.
- Am I creating wealth responsibly, using it to serve others, and taking care of myself and my relationships as I take this journey?

5. Principle of Making Friends With Death

There's no guarantee that I will make it until tomorrow or even to my next breath.

- From traveling in South Africa and India, three years as a hospice volunteer in San Francisco, and practicing the teachings of the Buddha, I practice living each day as my last.
- I'm kind as often as possible (to others and to myself). I tell people that I love them. And I keep a tiny smile on my face to keep my outlook (and my mind) light.

6. Principle of Personal Responsibility

All people want to be happy, healthy, safe, and secure (just like you and me), so I practice making choices that are aligned with my principles and are an expression of who I am. (And I pay attention to how others respond.)

- I recognize that every person creates their reality and experiences based on habits, conditioning, history, beliefs, attitudes, and choice.
- Because of this, I take 100% responsibility for my experiences and practice not taking them personally.
- I have the power to make a new choice.
- I am not afraid to say, "I'm sorry."
- I realize that each person is responsible for their thoughts, words, choices, actions, and experience.

7. Principle of Compassionate Service

I recognize the immense suffering in the world. At the same time, I recognize that I can help.

- Through empathy (allowing myself to experience another person's situation by seeing the world through their eyes), I cultivate compassion which gives me the energy, inspiration, and lightness of heart to serve.
- From there, I no longer focus on the suffering and problems but shift my focus to opportunity and solutions. And smile.

May these 7 Principles of Influence With A Heart® inspire you, challenge you, make you smile, and serve you in the best possible ways... especially as you write your book!

An Open Invitation For Us To Chat

Do you want to get your book done in just 5 weeks? Do you want to create more influence and impact?

If so, I'd love to chat with you!

I'll spend about 30 minutes with you, and I'll ask you a series of questions so you can get clear on your next best steps. We'll see if writing your book in 5 weeks is the right strategic move for you, right now.

Helping you get clear is my superpower. That's why consultants, coaches, speakers, and solopreneurs come to me—so they can 10X their influence and impact.

During this call, I'll help you get clear on your next best steps. (Writing a book isn't for everyone.)

You getting clear is good for all of us, and it's what the world needs. So whether you get your book done with me in just 5 weeks—or not—it will be an honor and a privilege to support you in getting clear on what's next.

So join me for a no-strings, no-hassle call by choosing a convenient time that works best for you at InfluenceWithAHeart.com/connect today.

Remember the power of your book. You'll be positioned as an expert, authority, thought leader, or influencer who people know, like, and trust.

So when people invest in your training, service, product, or program—and get behind you and your vision—they will be even more invested in their success (and therefore yours).

(And then imagine what will happen when you inspire more people to say yes to you and to your stuff!)

There's no need to wait. Because you're going to die. All of us are. And we have no idea when.

So isn't your time—right now?

Email ben@influencewithaheart.com, join my network on Linked at influencewithaheart.com/LinkedIn, or visit InfluenceWithAHeart.com/connect to schedule a convenient time for a free consultation with me.

I look forward to speaking with you soon—and am honored to support you as you create more influence, income, impact, and a wonderful legacy with your business!

Cheers,

Ben

The Framework: Influence With A Heart®

As you know:

1. You can 10X your influence and impact by writing a book that changes businesses and lives.

2. This means using more empathy, story, and thought leadership—plus a dash of loving-kindness. (By doing this, you automatically use the key principles of psychological influence from a place of service and compassion.)

3. It's the same approach whether you're communicating with 1, 10, or 10,000 people and whether you're online, onstage, on the phone, or face-to-face.

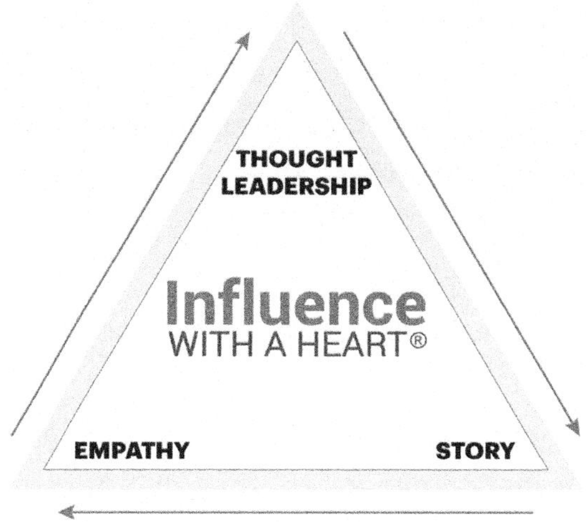

This Is How And Why It Works

LOVING-KINDNESS

1. Often know as metta, loving-kindness is the wish and intention for yourself (and all beings) to be happy, safe, peaceful, and free. Loving-kindness happens when you relax your head, relax your face, smile, and feel the love in your heart. Then you share it by smiling at others.

EMPATHY

1. Empathy allows you to see the world through another person's eyes and connect with them from a place of authenticity, integrity, and service.

2. Empathy helps you understand and have compassion for people's fears, frustrations, needs, desires, aspirations, goals, and dreams. It also helps you make better informed choices and take more effective approaches to multiple situations in your business.

3. What this means is that you will discover:

   - The best ways you can help your clients, customers, colleagues, or audience

- What language to use to communicate with them
- How to give and receive feedback (skillfully)
- What messaging, products, and services to create
- How to deliver powerful, transformative value that will impact people's business or life—or both

4. Empathy invites people to realize that you're an authentic thought leader, expert, authority, or influencer who truly cares about them.

As a result, they're inspired to tell others about you!

STORY

1. Stories reach people's hearts as well as their minds. So your stories create inspiration by creating an emotional experience for your reader or listener.
   - While logic and facts are important, emotion is what moves people to action.
2. Stories help you express your unique purpose and create a vivid vision of the future, to help your business succeed.

- Stories allow people to see the world through your eyes and stand in your shoes
- Stories get everyone on the same page

3. Your story helps you express your unique purpose and who you are. As a result, you develop more clarity, confidence, and magnetism so more of the right people will respond to you.

4. Stories (about you, your clients, etc.) help people know you, like you, trust you, and want to develop an ongoing relationship with you. You create an almost instant rapport with your audience, listener, or reader.

THOUGHT LEADERSHIP

1. Thought leadership comes from your "special sauce". This is your years of experience, discovery, hard-earned wisdom, education, "failures," triumphs, anecdotes, mishaps, joys, insights, training, investments, wisdom, time, energy, and love.

2. You walk the path that you're guiding others along. You offer a blueprint, framework, or roadmap so others can create their own version of success.

3. You create powerful connections and referrals.

4. You have a clear message and unique offer that connects to what your ideal clients want.

5. Your Key Positioning Currency (KPC) is clear, consistent, and current, including:

    1) Your LinkedIn summary and tagline
    2) Your 100-word intro for referrals, interviews, podcasts, etc.
    3) Your elevator pitch and expertise framework
    4) You know how to talk about the value of your offer (10X) so more people say YES(!) to you

In summary, this is:

1. YOU inspiring and inviting people to change their thoughts so they can choose to change their behaviors and take action that's good for them and good for you!

2. YOU offering unique perspectives, tools, techniques, possibilities, and transformation to your clients, customers, colleagues, or audience!

3. YOU making a bigger impact, make your business more successful, and help move the world forward!

Now that you understand the framework, let me tell you how *Influence With A Heart* started...

Ben's Story

I'd like to take just a few minutes and tell you my story because I'd like you to know who I am, where I've been, and what I'm all about. And to let you know where my insights and discoveries have come from.

So take a moment, take a deep breath, smile, and imagine me trekking in the mountains of southern India with a guide named Vijay (who had a really big smile).

At 6,000 feet up, it was hot, dry, and dusty because it hadn't rained in four months. The sun was beating down on our heads and shoulders, and Vijay was telling me his story as we walked together along the path.

All of a sudden, from behind the trees (where I couldn't see anything), I could hear screams and shouts (not in English, of course). And then Vijay yelling, "Run!" over his shoulder as he ran off down the path.

So I ran. And ran. And ran...

I didn't know why I was running, but I knew that I was running for my life!

And this was already the second time—out of four times, in just 72 hours—that I almost died in India.

As I kept running along this dry and dusty mountain path, my life started flashing before my eyes.

- I remembered my childhood, then high school in New York City (mostly), and then college where I earned a BA in psychology and a BA in creative writing

- I remembered producing magazines (that were published by Hearst and Condé Nast) and working with a variety of startups and traveling in 16 countries

- I remembered helping to launch *AARP The Magazine* (that was mailed to 32 million people)

- I remembered helping two chapters of The ALS Association through an organizational consolidation so they could serve half the people in California living with Lou Gehrig's disease (a few years before The Ice Bucket Challenge)

- Then I remembered that one fateful day when I realized something that would change the entire course of my life: I was fed up and discouraged

- I was fed up with the business world because everything I could see was focused on profit at the expense of everything and everyone else

- I was discouraged with nonprofits because I could see that most didn't have the power, knowledge, training, or resources to make a bigger impact (even though so many nonprofits and NGOs do incredible things)

So that's when it dawned on me: Hey, I want to make a bigger impact with my business and be part of making an ongoing, major, positive shift on the planet!

So I chose to help the individuals, companies, organizations, and movements that are already making a difference, those that want to "turn up the volume" on their influence, income, and impact.

With this clarity, I focused on becoming a top-notch leader, coach, marketer, and communicator. I also started a regular meditation practice that I've been doing since 2006 (including 119+ days of silent retreats so far).

I spent years synthesizing everything I'd learned, created, and achieved: at school, in the corporate world, in the nonprofit world, and in my life. I studied with incredible coaches.

I joined masterminds with influential people and learned from powerful mentors. I studied genius copywriters. I read tons of books, took lots of courses, and took lots and lot of notes.

- The more I learned, the more action I took
- More action meant more feedback; more feedback meant more clarity
- More clarity meant (and means) more results

I also made lots (and lots) of mistakes! So I reflected on all of these "failures," learned the lessons (some really hard ones), and cultivated my own wisdom and insights.

I was then able to take all of this knowledge plus hard-earned wisdom and use it as a strategic (and philosophical) roadmap to launch my first consulting business.

I wrote a #1 best-selling book called *Marketing With A Heart: How To Use Trust Based Marketing For Greater Income, Influence, and Impact*. I followed with another best-selling book, *Influence With A Heart: How To Be A Better Leader and Communicator by Using More Empathy, Story, and Thought Leadership*.

Today, I'm privileged, grateful, and blessed to help people write a high-quality book (in just 5 weeks) and then publish and position themselves for a media explosion in three months!

Still Wondering How I Almost Died Four Times?

If you're still wondering how I almost died 4 times in 72 hours in India, here's what happened:

#1 was when my bus completely demolished a guardrail and almost went over the edge, as it skidded around the tight curve of windy mountain road

#2 was when my guide, Vijay, and me were running and running and running from an out-of-control, blazing forest fire

#3 was when we stumbled upon a snake—small, green, and deadly—on the path in front of us

(Thank goodness for Vijay because I didn't see it!)

#4 was encountering a mountain lion (that somehow, miraculously, ran off)

That entire, terrifying, eye-opening, nerve-racking experience was perhaps the best 72 hours of my life! It gave me a gift: an overflowing gratitude for life and a fire inside to create massive, positive impact.

That's why you and I are both here today. So let's dig in!

Chapter 1:
START WITH SELF-CARE:
Loving Kindness, Meditation, Forgiveness, and Letting Go

Summary: START WITH SELF-CARE

1. Meditation and mindful awareness offer a wealth of proven results for individuals and organizations, including:

    - More innovation
    - Better engagement
    - Improved resilience
    - Greater happiness
    - Higher performance
    - Decreased absenteeism
    - Better communication
    - Improved health and well-being
    - Greater profitability

2. Practicing forgiveness can help you be more receptive to ideas and insights while cultivating your ability to engage with what's happening in a more focused, vibrant, and nonjudgemental way.

3. Part of achieving your goals and dreams comes from self-care habits like optimizing your morning, your day, and how you do your work. It's just as important to remember that success also comes from learning how to keep letting go of what no longer serves you.

Meditation Is Not New, and People Are Finally Catching On To The Goodness It Offers

More and more businesses are bringing meditation and mindfulness practices into the workplace, while more people are meditating at home and sharing awareness practices with their family, friends, and children.

If you do a quick search on the web, you'll find articles on CNN Money, Forbes, Huffington Post, Bloomberg Business—as well as multiple, reputable academic sources—about meditation, mindful awareness, and how they contribute to success and happiness.

These practices can help coaches and consultants, speakers and solopreneurs, entrepreneurs, executives, and visionary leaders become:

1. Better aligned with their higher purpose

2. Flexible, adaptive, responsive, and resilient with what's happening and changing around them

3. More effective in their thinking, decisions, and ability to create and share value

4. More understanding of themselves and (as a result) more confident, capable, and authentic

I've been sitting meditation and practicing mindful awareness regularly since 2006. I couldn't live without them. Let me rephrase: I wouldn't live without them because they are effective in:

1. Staying healthier (mentally, physically, emotionally)

2. Being more flexible, creative, and innovative

3. Reducing anxiety, stress, doubt, and worry

4. Dealing with physical and emotional pain

5. Managing grief, impatience, and anger

6. Navigating in a rapidly changing world

7. Supporting this amazing, challenging, delightful adventure that is both my business and my life

The most effective meditation is metta (loving kindness). How? Put a tiny smile on your face and gently hold your awareness on the feeling/sensation of love in your heart. Then allow that feeling to radiate out in all directions (no effort, just like the light of a candle).

When you get distracted, relax your head, relax your face, smile, and come back to the feeling of love in your heart.

How to Quit Suffering Now (a.k.a. The Buddha Smile, My Signature Talk)

Four times.

In three days.

FOUR TIMES IN THREE DAYS!

That's how many times I faced death on a hike in southern India.

I walked away from that experience with two huge gifts: gratitude for my life and a deeper connection to my purpose.

I thought these gifts were enough for me to finally be happy. Boy, was I ever wrong.

Two years later, I'm back in India—for my second hike—and still looking for happiness.

Now picture me (with a long beard)—in the Himalayas—12,000 feet up—with mountain peaks more than twice that height all around.

This time, I'm receiving more gifts!

Jolting pain with every step I took because of the blisters. One on each foot (from getting my boots fixed in India instead of showing up with new ones).

And jolting pain from my incessant, inner dialogue.

("Dumb ass!")

With every step, I was angry, judgmental, and full of regret. Clearly, the pain wasn't enough.

I was adding lots of self-hatred and guilt for all the years of parties, pills, and white powders.

Each miserable step launching me back in time to that first hike when I was terrified that I would die—violently—and far, far from home.

1. Starting with my bus almost going off the side of a mountain (as I literally swung out over the abyss)

2. Next, I'm running from a wildfire

3. Then, almost stepping on a poisonous snake

4. And finally, crossing paths with a mountain lion that (somehow) ran away first

And you know what? I was high as a kite the whole time!

Ganja—a Sanskrit word for marijuana—is an offering to the Hindu God, Shiva.

I was offering lots to Shiva, all day, almost every day.

Because for most of my adult life, I was trying to stop my own suffering.

But so far, not doing a good job.

Clearly.

I remember being home after surviving that first hike.

Still suffering. Still looking for happiness. So I start smoking meth.

(But don't worry, it was only on Friday nights.)

At least in the beginning.

For the next two years, my relationships sucked, I lost a few jobs, and I withdrew every last penny from my 401(k).

My life—a magnificent mess!

Then, my birthday finds me outside, imploring the Universe, "I just want to be free!"

And five months later I'm back in India—for my second hike.

Now—instead of dying—I'm facing something equally profound.

With every step. All 144,000 steps.

For 9 days straight. For 8 hours a day.

Jolting pain, and my inner voice repeating like a dog chasing its tail.

("You suck. You came back to get your shit together, and all you have are two stupid blisters.")

Which I began noticing right around the three-hour mark on day one.

Now, it's lunchtime. I'm hangry! And weeping and cursing myself while shoving food in my face.

If there had been a freezer full of Ben & Jerry's...

Now, I'm using my knife to "unfix" my shoes...

Then wrapping my ankles in moleskin and gauze, which ain't gonna do a damn thang.

And I'm realizing that all I can do is keep walking forward.

Then, day five—something starts happening!

As I'm walking, I'm seeing the epic majesty of these 28,000-foot peaks, and I'm—HAPPY!

And starting to hear the words from the whispers walking beside me.

Like the dawn, lighting up the mountain tops.

PROCLAIMING in glorious language...

"Dude, you're in the present moment."

("Holy crap. I am!")

I feel my body relax, a tiny smile in my heart.

And I figure it out (albeit twelve years later)!

By smiling, my body relaxes. And suddenly the pain of each step—is just pain.

I'd just planted a seed that would help me discover the meditation practice that would teach me how to quit suffering.

I call it The Buddha Smile.

Just like the Buddha, I realized that pain doesn't have to become suffering.

Let me say that differently.

Suffering is an outcome. Suffering happens when you add things like anger, worry, regret, and judgment to your pain, whether it's a broken promise, a broken toe, or even a broken heart.

Not only do you create your own suffering, you multiply it for yourself and the people around you.

Which makes your "suffering habit" even stronger.

So I'm here to say, QUIT IT. You don't have to suffer anymore!

And the good news is that you don't need to meditate for twelve years like I did or go halfway or around the world or trek through the Himalayas with blisters to take this gift home with you.

- The fact that you're hearing my voice means that you're already receiving it.
- Now imagine what your life looks like as you keep understanding this.
- Then imagine what life looks like when the whole world gets it!

When people realize that pain is just pain and that we all have the power to stop suffering.

RIGHT NOW.

When you quit suffering, you create so much more time, energy, and inspiration. You literally have more life!

So I invite you to ask yourself, What can I do—RIGHT NOW—to be happier?

(And remember. It all starts with a smile.)

###

Forgiveness Meditation Instructions (Brief)

This a soft, gentle way of learning how to lovingly accept whatever arises and to let it be, without trying to control it with your thoughts. (It's not for pushing things away.)

- As you sit quietly (eyes closed), repeat the phrase, I forgive myself for:
    - not understanding;
    - making this/these mistakes; and
    - causing pain to myself or anyone else.
- Then you shift your focus to another person by using and repeating the phrase, I forgive you for... (same as above).
- Finally, imagine hearing the other person saying these words to you, I forgive you for... (same as above).

You may feel mental, physical, or emotional discomfort during this process. That's okay. Try not to take it personally.

Simply relax your head, relax your face, and put that tiny smile back on your face. (This helps the forgiveness practice by keeping your mind light.)

Repeat as necessary and allow the changes to happen.

Drinking Coffee and Being Mindful About It

The experience of getting ready to drink a cup of coffee (or whatever you love) captures the essence and power of mindful awareness.

###

Coffee!

Do you remember that moment?

Let me take you there.

You feel a flutter of excitement in your belly as you hand your menu back to the server.

Coffee is coming!

You know it.

And you can already smell it.

You're aware of yourself as you look around at your surroundings and at the other diners as they eat breakfast.

You take a few, deep, nourishing breaths as you recognize some familiar faces. It's nice to see people you know.

As you hear the sounds of forks and knives gently hitting the plates nearby, it's clear that many people already have their coffee.

Coffee!

- You notice a twinge of jealousy toward the other patrons as well as impatience at your server (and the cook that you can't see) because you don't have your coffee yet.

- Then you acknowledge that sometimes your mind just churns out stories like these and you don't need to buy in to the noisy, negative, incessant chit-chat.

- You also realize that you're happy because you know what it's like to experience, enjoy, and be grateful for the gift of coffee.

And it's coming soon!

So you take a moment, take a few deep breaths, and then smile.

Because the kitchen door just opened, and here comes coffee!

You know that dark deliciousness is about to dazzle your palate.

So you offer thanks (and perhaps a little affirmation or prayer) for all of the great things in your life. Like coffee.

And then, you take a sip.

Coffee!

• • •

The preceding "coffee experience" is one way of describing mindful awareness in action.

It doesn't mean that drinking coffee is a guarantee that you'll be mindful.

Nor does it mean that you must drink coffee to be mindful.

It does mean that you can practice mindful awareness in every moment of your day (and get the benefits) while at work and home, no matter what you're doing.

The real definition of mindfulness (from the Buddha, in the Suttas, not the Commentaries) is being aware of the movement of mind's attention as it moves from one thing to another.

So this coffee experience illustrates ten examples of mind's attention as it moves:

1. Intentionally remembering an event or experience

2. The present-moment physical awareness of yourself:

    a. Via the sensations in your body
    b. The movement of your arm as you give the menu to the server
    c. The feeling of being in contact with your seat

3. Acknowledging a piece of information (coffee is coming)

4. Recognizing that you're anticipating an event (coffee is coming)

5. Being cognizant that you're smelling coffee

6. Breathing and knowing that you're doing it as you're doing it

7. Your awareness of yourself, your physical surroundings, ambient sounds, people around you, and feeling good because it's nice to see folks you know

8. Remembering that your mind is a "thought factory" that pumps out a lot of noise (on top of, and in spite of, your wisdom and insights)

9. Offering gratitude to honor and acknowledge your blessings

10. Being present as you take your first sip

What comes next?

- Some people go out for breakfast (regardless of the time) or make a pot of coffee right away

- Others consider how they can bring more mindful awareness and meditation into their communication, into their leadership, and into their lives

What comes next for you?

Creating Success by Telling Yourself a Story

Everything that humans create begins in the mind and the heart: inspiration and insight coupled with passion, intention, and the desire to bring things to life.

Put another way, what we think, say, and do creates our reality (in that order).

Uncountable numbers of scientists, leaders, athletes, spiritual masters, and high performers have proven this.

That's why so many people who are committed to achieving their goals and dreams dedicate time, energy, and intention to envisioning and affirming success.

Whether it's winning a gold medal, public speaking, writing a book, or self-healing, the power of affirmative thinking, imagination, and visualization is astounding.

I want to invite you into a brief imagination and visioning exercise (five steps).

1. Start by smiling and taking a couple of deep breaths. Take a few moments to connect to your unique sense of purpose

2. Imagine you've succeeded in every way you want (don't limit yourself)

3. Feel in your heart and body what that will do for you, your business, and the people you serve!

4. Hold that beautiful, powerful vision—and the feeling of the future you want—in your awareness for two or three breaths

5. Now, create your story, smile, and visualize what you want to happen, happening successfully (whether in the next three minutes, the next three months, or the next three years)

Whether you're preparing to make an offer, learn a skill, play a game of tennis, or follow your morning ritual, imagine yourself doing it (successfully) before you do it. Because what you do and what you think about doing are the same thing as far as your brain is concerned.

This is why Olympic athletes invest lots of time imagining themselves winning the gold.

Think of a high diver. Not only does she picture herself making the perfect dive and landing in the water without making a splash...

She also pictures herself at the moment the gold medal is being placed around her neck, and she can hear the resounding applause from the audience as a tear rolls down her cheek.

Your brain functions the same way. You can visualize your own success. It's best when you use as many of your five senses as possible and with lots of emotion!

I invite you to take 60 seconds and try it out right now.

1. What's something that you want to achieve?
2. When you're imagining it, what do you see?
3. What do you hear?
4. What do you taste or smell?
5. What can you feel?
6. What are the emotions underneath, as you're imagining yourself experiencing success, reaching your goals, or achieving your dreams?
7. How do you picture yourself celebrating your success?

Pretty cool, huh? You're literally re-mapping your brain and rewiring your subconscious mind.

Now that you see how easy it is, below are three great times during your day for visualizing success. You can visualize your success for one, five, or fifteen minutes.

Remember, there's an important perspective to keep in mind: 5 minutes = 1/3 of 1% of your day.

That's only 0.35% of your entire day to craft your success and create the life you want!

1. Before bed. Look back on the day. Smile and let yourself feel satisfied. Imagine tomorrow's success.

2. In the morning. Visualize having a successful day, one where you do great work, serve lots of people, and have lots of fun! Imagine your day moving seamlessly from one pleasant experience to the next.

3. Before each part of your day. Imagine quick, effective, enjoyable, and fulfilling success. Anticipate the challenges and solutions to move beyond them.

While visualizing your future is a powerful way to help you succeed—since you're imprinting your subconscious with the images of the future you want—you want to spend the vast majority of your time here and now, in the present moment with meditation and mindful awareness.

One Success Habit Made Famous, Thanks to One Historical American President

I have a story for you, about a young man who was alive more than 150 years ago.

That's the 1800s, as a matter of fact.

Back then, certain things hadn't been invented yet. There were no cellphones. Actually, there were no phones at all. He died one year before the first phone call.

There was no internet, of course.

But there was this certain young man.

He came from a poor family, and his mother died when he was a small child.

From her teaching and example, there were two important things he learned, remembered, and practiced in his life.

The first (which his mother is said to have shared with her family on her deathbed) was, "Be good to one another."

The second was discipline.

Now, this is not the kind of discipline that most people think of when they hear that word. This is not a punishment, a "time out," or "you're in trouble." This is the kind discipline that is the foundation of success.

It was the kind of discipline that would create the thoughts, behaviors, and ultimately the habits that helped this young man succeed. And he did truly amazing things.

According to some people, he's famous for saying this:

"If I had six hours to chop down a tree, I'd spend the first four hours sharpening the axe."

After you've let this quote sink in, take a moment and think about your week.

You go to work (or work from home), learn lots of new information, process new ideas, interact with different people, try to get in some exercise, and still have time to savor this gift of life and spend time with the people you love. (And get plenty of sleep and eat right, too.)

Are you actually able to do all that?

If the answer is no, don't go beating yourself up. Maybe you just never learned how to sharpen your axe.

(At this point, you might be saying, "But I don't even have an axe!")

That's okay. Because the "axe" is your mind.

And you sharpen it by creating habits.

Good habits.

When you create (and maintain) good habits, lots of good things can happen for you very quickly.

Here are three of those good things:

1. You focus and pay attention to what you're doing for longer, so you stop getting distracted. This means you get more done than ever before, faster.

2. You have less stress and anxiety, sleep better, and feel healthier.

3. You achieve more with less effort and have more fun with what you're doing so you can reach your biggest goals and dreams while having the life you want today.

Are you ready to sharpen your axe?

If so, it's simply a matter of taking on one new habit and doing it each day.

Here's the one habit: create a morning ritual that you love, and do it daily.

Your morning ritual sets the tone for success as you care for your body, mind, and spirit. This is where you start sharpening the axe so you can have an amazing day.

Here's an example:

- Eating a healthy breakfast (15 minutes)
- Making your bed (2 minutes)
- Reading something inspiring (5 minutes)
- Drinking 16 ounces of water (3 minutes)
- Meditating (10 minutes)
- Exercising (20 minutes)
- (55 minutes total)

Imagine doing all of this before you even leave the house or start your work. How do you imagine your day will go?

Important: When you create your morning ritual, do the same things in the same order every day.

This will make it easier to do since you won't have to spend time or energy thinking or making choices.

You can save your energy and willpower for innovation, success, creativity, and the surprises that will happen throughout the day.

(Inspired by Hal Elrod's book, *Miracle Morning*.)

Oh, I almost forgot.

This young man, the one with the axe, in case you were still wondering.

That was Abraham Lincoln.

He kept sharpening his axe.

Look what he did, and how many people he impacted in his lifetime and beyond.

Now, imagine what your business and your life will be like when you keep sharpening your axe!

Learning How to Keep Letting Go So You Can Be Happier and Make the Impact You Want

The things we experience—with others, in the world around us, and with ourselves—are impacted by our interpretations, expectations, assumptions, intentions, beliefs, biology, principles, values, environment, associations, fears, and desires.

That's a lot of input that can keep us from seeing the truth and the reality of the world around us and within ourselves.

For as much as we all must keep learning and understanding and discovering—there's as much, if not more, that we need to unlearn and release—so we can grow, succeed, and create more influence in the world.

And so we can love who we are and what we're about, every single day.

Otherwise, our ability to make a bigger impact and live the life that we love is limited by the roles, stories, and beliefs that have been handed to us, rather than what we've discovered for ourselves.

Wisdom, joy, and magic show up in our lives when we let things go.

Did you ever stop and think about all the learning that's happened in your life?

So much learning, so much information, so many experiences.

So much stuff, and some might be holding you back.

Holding you back from yourself, your greatness, your happiness, doing the work you love (on your own terms), and living your life the way you want to live it.

- It might be what you learned at school and what you learned from your parents and friends
- What (many of us) learned from television
- There's what the internet teaches
- What work teaches
- What your mistakes and misperceptions teach
- What debt and scarcity thinking teach
- What religion and spirituality teach
- What altered states of consciousness teach

- What our spouses or partners teach
- What our children teach
- What our pets teach
- What sickness, old age, and death teach

That's a lot of teaching, from when you were young and very impressionable to today, where you are less impressionable, a bit wiser, and more discerning.

All of us have values and beliefs that we never chose for ourselves, but somehow, they became a part of us.

And part of the business world.

And that's usually what holds us back.

So what's one thing you can surrender, right now?

From there, what do you want to cultivate more of as you take your business (and your life) to the next level?

What are you going to do for yourself, for your business, and your life, so you can make a bigger impact?

Chapter 2: EMPATHY

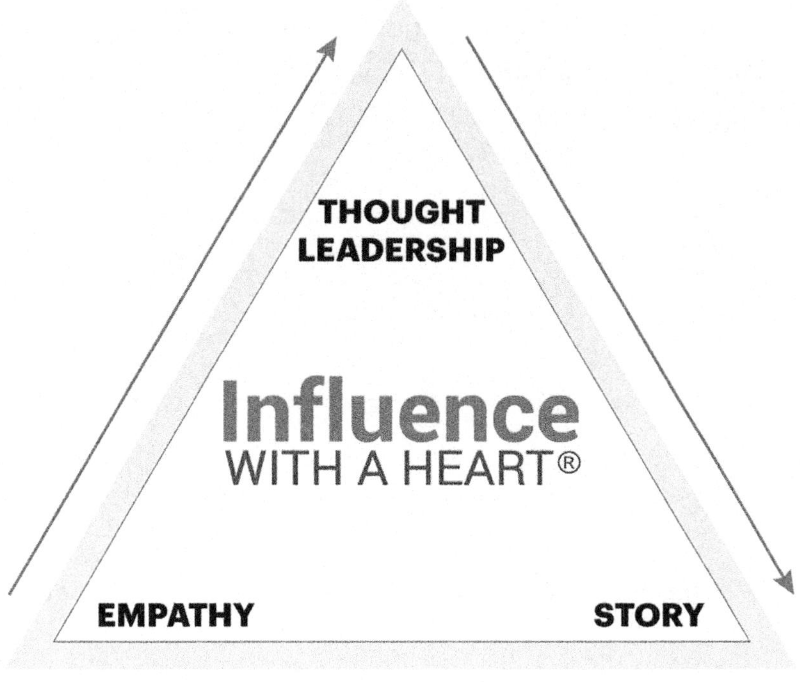

Summary: EMPATHY

1. Empathy allows you to see the world through another person's eyes and connect with them from a place of authenticity, integrity, and service.

2. Empathy helps you understand and have compassion for people's fears, frustrations, needs, desires, aspirations, goals, and dreams. It also helps you make better informed choices and take more effective approaches to multiple situations in your business.

3. What this means is that you will discover:

    - The best ways you can help

    - What language to use to communicate with them

    - How to give and receive feedback (skillfully)

    - What messaging, products, and services to create

    - How to deliver powerful, transformational value

As a result, they're inspired to tell others about you!

Influence Is About Shaping the Future, So Connect the Dots and Make Your Vision Clear

Whether you're an executive, entrepreneur, speaker, author, coach, trainer, consultant, or other visionary—who's committed to making a positive change in the world—you are a leader.

You're a leader because you are shaping the future as well as your own reality. You're bringing your vision, story, message, idea, product, or service to the world.

Because of this, it's critical to communicate with people in a way that educates and inspires them to take action.

Connect the dots from your vision to their goals and dreams. Don't assume they'll get it. Make the path clear.

(This is because you're competing with so much noise and distraction that we all face every day.)

Do this with your prospects, customers, clients, vendors, partners, managers, stockholders, co-workers, employees, government, media, communities, and your board of directors.

Everyone your business touches.

Apparently, there are lots of different groups here with an astounding array of goals, challenges, fears, pains, hopes, desires, and dreams. Keep connecting the dots.

Important: you can't talk to all of these people about the same things or use the same language.

1. Instead, begin with empathy: get to know your audience and speak to them in their language about the things that are most important to them.

2. Ask people to share their stories with you, so you can understand even more of what's going on for them. Ask questions. Ask more questions. Go deep.

3. Tell people your story so they have the chance to know, like, and trust you while seeing you as the expert, thought leader, authority, or leader that you truly are.

When you take these three steps, the magic happens.

You understand them, they understand you, and you have everything you need for influence, leadership, marketing, communication, and authentic human connection that creates real transformation.

And your book is a great way to make it happen but remember about the psychology.

Using the Psychology of Influence (Ethically)

An amazing resource about the psychology of influence is a book called *Influence* by Robert Cialdini. You'll understand how and why people say yes—and then how to use these insights (ethically) in your business. You'll learn the six principles of influence: knowing, liking, trust, authority, reciprocity, and consistency.

Use these every time you communicate, then people will know you, like you, trust you, and see you as an expert or authority. They will invest in you, get behind you, and give you the opportunity to serve them.

Always remember the three things that motivate people and inspire them to take action:

1. They want to achieve happiness and avoid suffering
2. They want to overcome their internal struggles of self-doubt, fear, worry, anxiety, or insecurity
3. They want greater meaning, purpose, and connection in a rapidly changing world that's in a vast and mysterious universe

Start using more empathy, today, and you will love what happens!

How Well Do You Know Who You're Talking To?

If you want to connect and develop a trusting relationship with your prospect, customer, client, colleague, or audience, you'll want to communicate in their language about the things that are the most important to them.

This means using the exact words and phrases they use when they describe their challenges, fears, frustrations, needs, experiences, hopes, goals, desires, and dreams.

Around the world, we speak different languages, practice different customs, and do different things. This is reality, and it occurs country to country, business to business, culture to culture, generation to generation, situation to situation, and person to person.

It's critical to get super clear on what's important to people—and how they talk about it—so you can create the most effective communication, rapport, and connection. To get started, do your research, talk to lots of people, and make sure you're as clear as possible with these three things:

1. Key data (demographics) that can be measured, such as gender, age, income, marital status, etc.—the "dry" (perhaps) and vitally important facts

about your clients, customers, employees, team, market, or audience

2. Group trends (psychographics) such as behaviors, hobbies, spending habits, values/principles, product usage, opinions, where they hang out online, interests, and lifestyle choices

3. Individual purpose and passion (sociographics) that go deep, giving you an understanding of what motivates people: their personal needs, attitudes, fears, frustrations, goals, dreams, and what gives meaning to their lives

Then you will connect with people on an emotional and experiential level, which is what you want. Then you have the right language for better marketing, more influential communication, creating tailored products/services, and leadership that creates transformation.

Again, remember those three things that motivate people:

1. They want to achieve happiness and avoid suffering

2. They want to overcome their internal struggles of self-doubt, fear, worry, anxiety, or insecurity

3. They're searching for greater meaning, purpose, and connection in a rapidly changing world in a vast and mysterious universe

Knowing as much of this information as possible will help you expand your sphere of influence as you discover other people who are connected to your prospect, client, customer, or audience.

This allows you to serve a wider range of people, businesses, or organizations.

Here's how to uncover this information:

- Ask questions about people's biggest challenges
- Do your research
- Email a survey to your list
- Make calls
- Give a talk
- Offer a webinar

- Start or participate in a LinkedIn group, mastermind group, or networking group that's aligned with you

The more that you know about your client/customer/audience/colleague/market—from their day-to-day experiences to the deep, emotional, "keep-you-up-at-night" details—the more successful you will be.

- You'll connect, communicate, and lead better

- You'll reach more people with your ideas and message

- You'll create a shared human connection and experience while getting people excited about who you are, what you're about, and how you're going to make an impact in their business or life—or both

- You'll create superior products and services that deliver exceptional value (based on what your people want and need because they've told you)

- You'll discover even more people like them to serve (since you've clearly articulated who you help and how you help them)

- You'll energize even more people with your vivid vision of the future and show them a way to get there

And writing your book is a great way to wrangle your thinking and wisdom into one place.

Because then you can repurpose the heck out of your book!

Elevating Your Elevator Pitch

Very often, opportunity starts with the question, "So, what do you do?"

Very often, you only have a few seconds to get—and then hold—a person's attention as you answer.

How do you do it? How do you hold this person's attention and give them the answer that clearly and effectively communicates the right combination of:

1) Who you help and how you help them

2) Who you are and why you care

3) A dash of your "special sauce" so they remember you

Hint: people may forget what you say and do, but they'll never forget the way they feel, thanks to you. (Inspired by the poet Maya Angelou.)

The first thing to do is start right there.

Connect with their emotions. Think of affecting the ways that people feel (ethically, of course).

Talk about the things might be on their mind.

Instead of focusing on yourself and what you want, focus on this other person: what they want or need and their experience (their struggle, dream, or both).

From there, remember, this not a pitch, it's a cascade.

(That's why I call it an "elevated" elevator pitch.)

Sadly, most people still think it's a pitch. And they treat it like a pitch. A one shot deal. The big "at bat." A home run or nothing. But they couldn't be further from the truth.

Because every yes is part of a series of yeses. And building interest (just like cultivating relationships) operates much the same way.

Think of dominoes.

Or most waterfalls.

You'll notice that often the water doesn't fall directly from the top to the bottom. The water cascades—from level to level, step to step—top to bottom. (Another analogy: On your first date, you don't usually ask your date to marry you.)

So (before) the next time you're asked, "What do you do?" consider your response.

What will you say—and in what sequence—so that:

1. This person will get to know, like, and trust you

2. You position yourself as a caring expert, influencer, authority, or thought leader

3. You connect the dots—from what they want and need—to who you are and what you offer

4. You keep sparking interest, so the person you're speaking with keeps asking you, "Tell me more!"

If you're not sure, simply go back to basics: people want to be seen, heard, and understood. The want to overcome their challenges and achieve their dreams. And for all this to happen, these people must know, like, and trust you.

(This has been going on since the beginning of time.)

So ask them to share a story (of themselves, an experience, a case study, a success, a challenge, etc.).

And then share a story about you with them.

When you do this, you create the cascade that allows this person to have their business or life impacted by who you are and what you offer.

[What Are Your Thoughts or Insights?]

Case Study: Your Book Will Change Your Life

OPPORTUNITY I was invited to teach a two-day training at Stanford University about the Influence With A Heart Method®. The audience: 126 seven-figure earning, global business leaders.

BACKGROUND I knew I needed to make an extra good impression, so I told the event planner that I would give each person a free, autographed copy of my new book!

SOLUTION I wrote my book in five weeks and arrived at the event with copies in hand.

RESULTS New business came my way almost immediately. One audience member discovered that I was coming to Australia later that year as a guest speaker at a different event on the Sunshine Coast.

So, they invited me to speak at their company headquarters in Sydney! Two days later, they asked me to do a second talk (the next day) to a Chinese-speaking audience through a translator!

Three months later, I'm confirming a six-figure contract with a Fortune 100 company. They'd asked me to help create a mindfulness and empathy video game—with MIT—for more than 20,000 customer experience employees around the world!

ACTION: Use More Empathy in All of Your Communication with These 5 Simple Steps

1. Imagine that the person you're communicating with is your best friend and someone who wants to be happy, safe, healthy, and free (just like you).

2. Have a heart-to-heart discussion and listen to them about their dreams and challenges, what keeps them up at night, what they can't get out of their heads, what they want and need, and what they want to achieve in their business and in their life.

3. Empathize with them, acknowledge their pain, and let them know that they are not alone; that it is okay, there is hope; and that you are the one who can help them (or you will teach them how to help themselves).

4. Show them how to get past their pain or challenge starting today and over the long haul, then teach them how to reach their dreams as quickly and effectively as possible (in a way that supports who they are).

5. (Based on your "discussion") capture this information:

- What words are they using?
- What information are they sharing with you?
- What emotions are coming up (them and you)?
- How are they describing their experience?
- What stories are they telling?

Now that you have these answers, use them (ethically) in all of your communications, starting today. Because five amazing things will happen:

First, you'll discover what's really going on in people's lives, what they're experiencing, what's motivating them (fears to dreams), and how you can best serve them.

Second, you'll have the language you need to speak (and write) to them. By using the exact words they use, you'll connect, deeply and authentically, with them.

Third, you'll automatically be positioned as the person who can help them. (Why? Because when you can articulate someone's pain, challenge, or dream in their own words—or even better than they would describe it—people often assume that you have the solution or that you can help them find it.)

Fourth, you'll know what products, services, or strategies to offer and how to position, package, and present them in a way that offers extreme value.

Fifth, it will help you create a community, tribe, or following of people who are committed to your vision.

Chapter 3: STORY

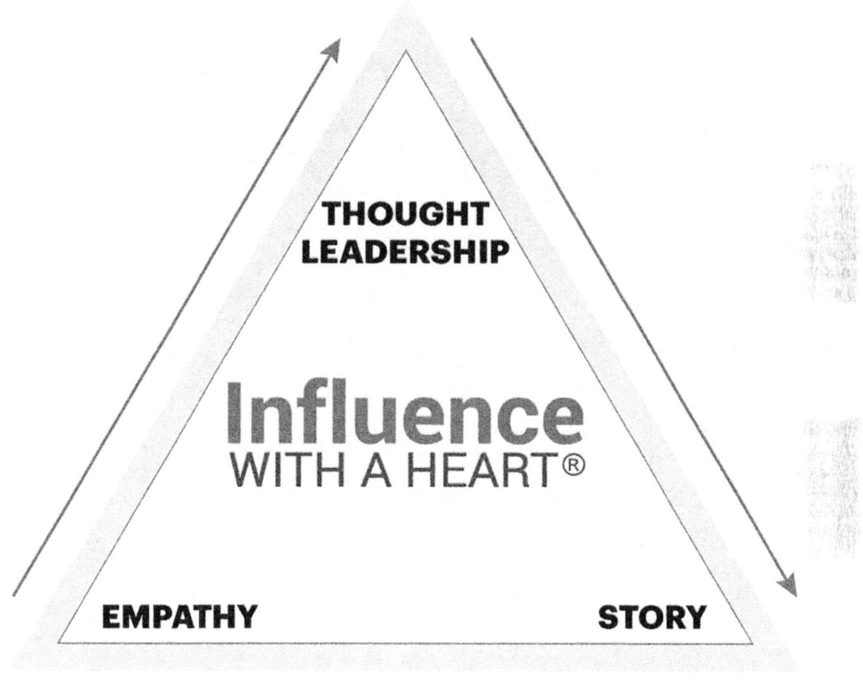

Summary: STORY

1. Stories reach people's hearts as well as their minds. So your stories create inspiration by creating an emotional experience for your reader or listener.

While logic and facts are important, emotion is what moves people to action. Put another way: Facts tell, emotions sell.

2. Stories help you express your unique purpose and create a vivid vision of the future to help your business succeed. Stories give other people the opportunity to see the world through your eyes and stand in your shoes.

They also help to get everyone on the same page with what's being communicated.

3. Your story helps you continue to discover your unique purpose and who you are. This helps you develop more clarity, confidence, and magnetism so more of the right people will respond to you.

4. Stories (about you, about your clients, etc.) help people know you, like you, trust you, and want to develop an ongoing relationship with you because they allow you to create an almost instant rapport with your audience, listener, or reader.

The Power of Story in Leadership

More than in any other time in history, our society and our businesses need leaders, the kind of leaders that care about the good of humanity and the planet.

You're a leader, whether you call yourself that or not. You're a leader, whether you're helping one person or changing the lives of millions.

Because real leadership isn't about titles. It's about caring for the people you serve and creating new realities in business, in your life, and in the world.

If you ask most high performers, self-development experts, brain scientists, and spiritual teachers, one of the fastest and most effective ways to create new realities (for yourself and others) is through stories.

Sharing your story—and discovering other people's stories—are key components of marketing to, communicating with, and leading a diverse array of people. (Essentially, you're creating new realities.) This can include any or all of the following:

1. Your prospects, customers, clients, audience

2. Your employees, vendors, partners

3. Managers, stockholders, co-workers, colleagues

4. The government, the media, your local community, and your board of directors

5. Basically, anyone (and everyone) that your business impacts

When you share your story, people will take an extra moment to read your words or hear what you say.

When you listen to their stories, these same people will realize that you understand and care about them.

- Stories make ideas and concepts tangible while making books fun to read, podcasts fun to listen to, and speeches fun to hear

- Stories are what helps make the learning stick so the things that you discover become part of your "muscle memory"

- Stories help you move folks from inspiration to action to satisfaction

- (You'll have an audience that will be hanging onto your every word, whether it's 1 or 10 or 10,000 people)

Stories don't have to take hours. You can tell a story in an instant with a gesture or with a smile. You can tell a story with an image, a handful of words, or a tweet. You can tell a story through video, email, or any medium that connects you to the people you serve.

This is so important, whether you're teaching, coaching, selling, serving, training, speaking, or leading.

Because you're inspiring people and connecting the dots from your vision to their goals and dreams. You're educating and influencing your audience to take action, so it benefits them and benefits you.

That's the power of story.

7 Things Happen When You Use Story

1. Stories will help get people to your website, onto your list, calling you for a consultation, investing in your products and services—and telling the world about what you offer—because it's changing their business or their life for the better.

2. Using more stories (including your signature story, case studies, client successes, testimonials, and even what you learned while riding the bus yesterday) will help make your business more

profitable so you can make a bigger impact. People will remember you because of the stories that you share.

3. You'll be influencing people to take action by appealing to reason and emotion.

4. When you discover and listen to someone else's story, you create an ongoing opportunity for them to know, like, trust, and see you as an expert, authority, influencer, or thought leader.

5. When you share your stories, people understand you and your vision and are inspired to follow your lead.

6. Although this is a world of different languages, cultures, and businesses, stories help people realize that we have much more in common than we have differences.

7. You'll be able to influence more lives every single day.

There isn't a social change, movement, or paradigm shift that's ever happened without stories. When there are no stories, no one listens.

But when you share your stories, people can't stop listening to you!

Your Story Is Your "Special Sauce"

Your story is an important part of who you are. Stories are the articulation of vision. Your story is your "special sauce": your years of experience, education, "failures", triumphs, anecdotes, mishaps, insights, investment, wisdom, time, energy, effort, talent, and everything in between.

Your stories can include any and all of the following:

1. Your signature story, "mess-to-success" moments, detours, and successes

2. Case studies and testimonials

3. Anecdotes about your colleagues, customers, clients, or audience

4. Their successes, challenges, goals, and dreams

5. Their experience of you or your company via your vision, idea, message, product, or service

6. Relevant bits of the news/science/history/literature/popular culture/an interesting that happened to you last week, etc.

7. Your purpose, guiding principles, and how you help make transformation and results happen

You have important stories. Your stories are key to what you offer to the world and the results that you bring to people's businesses and lives. That's valuable stuff!

- People will take an extra moment to read your words or hear what you're saying, as you share your story.

- Because stories make concepts and ideas real and tangible since they connect with people on an emotional level. I'll say it again: Stories reach people's hearts as well as their minds.

- Stories connect the dots between the perceptual and conceptual parts of your experience. And they make what you're saying so much more interesting!

It's one thing to hear or read the word "fruit."

It's a completely different experience when you hear about, read, or see an image of a red apple, in the hands of a smiling child who's getting ready to take another big bite as the juice is already running down her chin.

That's the power of story.

Stories are key, whether you're teaching, coaching, selling, serving, training, speaking, or leading. Because your story will help you connect the dots from your vision to people's goals and dreams.

Stories create opportunities for people to get to know you, while positioning you as the influencer, expert, authority, or thought leader that you are.

- This means that people will like you, trust you, and understand that you care about them and their experience.
- They'll realize that you truly see who they are, what they're facing, and what they most want to achieve.
- They'll know that you're the person who can help them get there and be delighted to say yes to you.

In essence, stories are one of the best ways to use Cialdini's six principles of influence.

When you share stories, here's what happens:

1. You'll establish the connection from a person's head to their heart

2. You'll inspire them to take action that's good for them and good for you

3. You'll have an audience that will hang onto your every word!

(That's why stories are good for your business.)

I always use stories in my teaching, coaching, writing, training, and speeches. Because—in a world with a dazzling array of cultures, customs, countries, language, dialects, geography, history, and politics—stories are the most direct method to bridge the gaps among different people.

- You can tell a story with an image or a picture, a handful of words, or even a tweet

- You can tell a story through video, email, or any communication medium that connects you to the people you serve

- You can tell a story in an instant with a gesture or with your smile

Stories give us the chance to speak from the heart and connect with the hearts of the people near us, across the country, and around the world!

Logic (Alone) Never Changed the World

One of the most important things I learned about being a better leader and communicator is how to mindfully choose how to respond to people, circumstances, events, and my own thoughts.

This all started in South Africa in 2002 and then continued in 2003 when I spent a few months traveling around the country, then living in Cape Town.

While I was there, I learned two things (thanks to Nelson Mandela) that inspired a transformation in my business and completely shifted my life.

The first thing I learned from Mandela (affectionately known as "Madiba") was about freedom.

It came from his example of how he responded to being locked up for 27 years in a South African prison, during apartheid.

All that time, he strove to keep his vision (his story) for a free South Africa alive.

The lesson: No matter what happens, you can choose to respond instead of reacting.

Think about it. The ways that people treat you are an outward expression of how they treat themselves. It has nothing to do with your value as a person.

That's a powerful truth.

And when you keep this truth on your radar, you immediately empower yourself.

You're more able to make a choice from moment to moment and to respond, rather than react.

You influence your capability (and therefore yourself) to make powerful choices more often.

For Madiba, this wasn't always easy. In fact, it was probably never easy.

But he kept at it because he knew that freedom starts on the inside.

He knew, just like we all know, that we're chock full of knee-jerk reactions just waiting to be unleashed.

Big ones, little ones, and everything-in-between ones.

But, in those beautiful moments...

when you can choose...

to make a conscious choice and respond...

you literally create freedom inside yourself!

Freedom from these four things:

1. Reaction (even if only for a moment)

2. Habit (the ones that no longer serve you)

3. The past

4. The future

Freedom is right now—in this one beautiful moment—a moment that's filled with all the seeds of possibility for something new, something different, and something better for the world and for yourself.

Something better for Mandela.

Twenty-seven years in prison under the apartheid regime, then he was elected president in 1994.

What an incredible journey, transformation, and example of unparalleled leadership!

Mandela (and the Story Continues)

If you take even a few minutes to learn more about Madiba, you'll see something amazing.

- One person who permitted himself to discover the gifts of an incredibly dark situation so he could influence his own life and the course of an entire country.

And this leads us to the second thing I learned from Madiba, which is also about freedom.

This time, it's the freedom that comes from forgiveness.

What happened under apartheid in South Africa resulted in violence and human rights abuses from all sides. No part of society escaped this.

So South Africa took a revolutionary approach to healing: truth, reconciliation, and the possibility of forgiveness on a large scale (through its Truth and Reconciliation Commission).

In a nutshell, the TRC offered public hearings where victims and survivors could share stories and confront former abusers (creating an opportunity for forgiveness and greater societal healing).

This powerful action (on a national level) showed me that it is possible to bring forgiveness into a larger arena.

Because when you start forgiving others, you create more freedom for yourself.

More forgiveness = more freedom

More freedom = more power

More power = more influence

More influence means that you and I can do even more great things in the world and make a bigger impact, whether it's helping 1 or 10 or 10,000 more people.

Because this road to freedom can be a long one:

1. In our hearts
2. In our minds
3. In the world around us

Remember, it's a marathon, not a sprint. And the only way we will get there is together.

So let's create a legacy that takes all of us there!

[What Are Your Thoughts or Insights?]

Case Study: It's Never Too Late for Your Book

OPPORTUNITY Mag Dimond, a woman in her 70s, was getting ready to publish her first book, *Bowing To Elephants, Tales of a Travel Junkie*. A brilliant writer, teacher, meditator, and philanthropist, she knew she needed help because the publishing industry has changed drastically in the last couple of decades.

BACKGROUND Mag knew she wanted to keep her focus on writing and speaking, not business development.

SOLUTION I began coaching her and consulting with a focus on launching, strategy, marketing, and messaging.

RESULTS Within six months, she was an international best seller, became an Editor's Pick for Elephant Journal magazine, won the IBPA Benjamin Franklin Award™ for the book's cover, was interviewed on more than 50 podcasts, and developed a large, vibrant Facebook community called Travels With Mag (almost 19,000 followers to date).

"I want to thank you, Ben, for your supportive coaching, intelligent strategizing, and your persistent and kind guidance... as we launched my #1 international, bestselling book, created the Writers Coming Together interview series, and will soon bring my new podcast, Bowing To Elephants, to the world!"

ACTION: Choose 13 of Your Best Stories by Using These 7 Guidelines

As you learned, "story" and "stories" can mean:

1. Your signature story, "mess-to-success" moments, detours, and successes

2. Case studies and testimonials

3. Anecdotes about your colleagues, customers, clients, or audience

4. Their successes, challenges, goals, and dreams

5. Their experience of you or your company via your vision, idea, message, product, or service

6. Relevant bits of the news/science/history/literature/popular culture/an interesting that happened to you last week, etc.

7. Your purpose, guiding principles, and how you help make transformation and results happen

How do you choose which stories to capture, clarify, and communicate? Remember that it all comes back to using more influence. You want to choose stories that:

1. Inspire people to change their ideas, change their minds, and make things happen

2. Are brimming with Cialdini's principles of influence

Your stories need to paint the pictures that allow your audience to know, like, and trust you while seeing you as a person who's in it for the "win-win." Here's how:

1. Choose three stories about yourself that clearly indicate you are a reliable source of information and a go-to person in your field

2. Come up with five brief anecdotes or illustrations that connect the dots from who you are and what you offer to the outcomes that people want

3. Think of all of your unique stories. What can you share that expresses you, the unique and wonderful you?

4. Capture a story that helped inspire your purpose or speaks to the beautiful heart that you have

5. Select your three biggest professional successes and write about them in a way that shows tangible outcomes

6. As you articulate any of these stories, draw upon other aspects of your life whether personal, professional, or anything between (without compromising your privacy, of course)

7. In creative writing classes, the professors teach, show, don't tell. So for our purposes, we want to show and tell.

So this means:

1. YES! Paint the pictures.

2. Make your stories multi-sensory (use as many of the five senses, plus emotion, as you are able).

3. Tell your reader, audience, or listener about the picture you just painted for them.

4. Speak, write, and connect from your heart as well as your mind. To do this, simply become aware of (or put your hand over) your heart (for just a moment) as you speak, write, connect, train, or teach.

5. Keep a file of these stories available and accessible.

And then watch to see how you impact people's lives!

Chapter 4:
THOUGHT LEADERSHIP

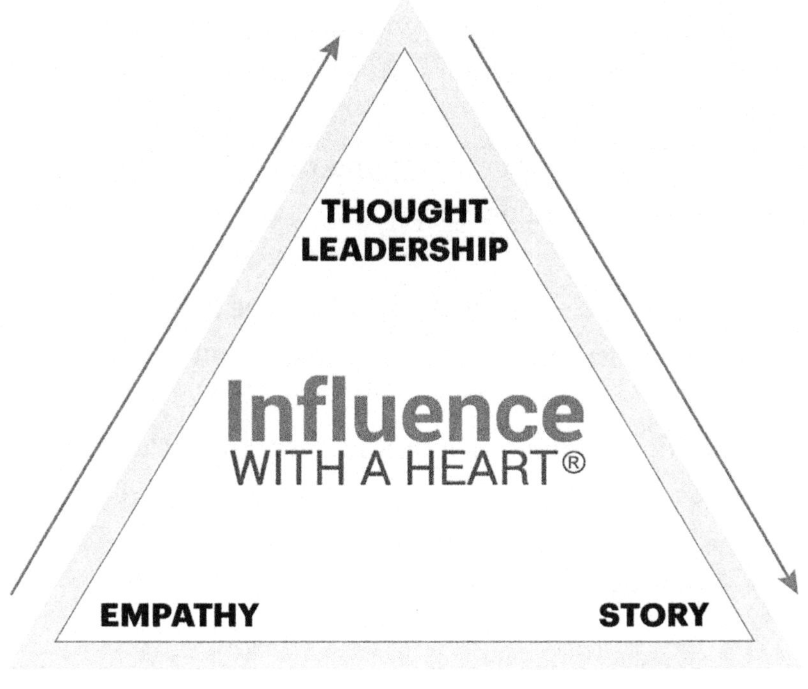

Summary: THOUGHT LEADERSHIP

1. Thought leadership comes from your "special sauce." This is your years of experience, discovery, hard-earned wisdom, education, "failures", triumphs, anecdotes, mishaps, joys, insights, training, investments, wisdom, time, energy, and love.

2. You walk the path that you're guiding others along. You offer a blueprint, framework, or roadmap so others can create their own version of success.

3. You create instant rapport and powerful, nourishing, sustainable connections.

4. You have a clear message and unique offer that connects to what your ideal clients want.

5. As a thought leader, your Key Positioning Currency (KPC) is clear, consistent, and current, including:

    A. Your LinkedIn Summary and Tagline
    B. Your 100-word intro for referrals, interviews, podcasts, and more
    C. Your elevator pitch and expertise framework
    D. How to talk about the value of your offer (10X) so more people (unhesitatingly) say, "YES!"

Thought Leadership Is Influence In Action and a Key Component of Your Story

Thought leadership is an interesting term. Lots of people use it. Lots of people claim that they are "thought leaders." Lots of people define it in lots of different ways.

For me—thought leadership is influence in action—and a key component of your story.

I was recently having a conversation with a new client, and she said something very interesting:

"I find that I have internal resistance to the idea of being a 'thought leader.' Somehow, I've created an image in my head of what 'real' thought leaders look like, and so I struggle with the notion of including myself in that group... "

The first thing I said (gently, and with so much love) was, "*Get over it.*" (We both laughed.)

Then I said, "*Okay, it's time to own your thought leadership (and your power) for these 7 reasons*:

1. "It's taking what you know, who you serve (and why), and your "special sauce"—and expressing that to your audience—whether you're online, onstage, on

the phone, or in person because you know it will help people with their business and in their life.

2. "Your thought leadership is uniquely yours because it's based on your years of experience, education, failures, triumphs, insights, investment, wisdom, time, energy, effort, talents—and everything between.

3. "Thought leadership is the part of your story that articulates your expertise, authority, capability, and leadership. People want to know these things about you.

4. "It will help you create a community, tribe, or following of people who are committed to your vision because they trust you, and you're helping them to realize their goals and achieve their dreams.

5. "It's an important part of inspiring people to take action because you're offering them new insights and perspectives while providing an evolving roadmap for success.

6. "These inspired people will literally become the voice of your company or organization and the ones who bring a flood of new and repeat business to your door.

7. "It will help you create and cultivate powerful relationships so you can move new ideas and possibilities from person to person, throughout organizations, throughout the world, and into the future."

Do you consider yourself a thought leader?

If you're not sure, then I invite you to take this 40-second quiz:

1. *"Am I a reliable source of information and a go-to person in my field of expertise?"*

2. *"Do I inspire people with innovative ideas?"*

3. *"Do I create relationships based on trust?"*

4. *"Do I turn my ideas into success, and can I show others how to replicate that success?"*

5. *"Am I known for making a difference in one person's life? Several lives? In my organization? In my world?"*

Now, based on your answers, are you a thought leader? (I would guess yes.)

Yes, you are a thought leader. If you want to be perceived as one, simply use more thought leadership every time you communicate.

How to Stand Out Authentically and Uniquely

Think of your positioning as the articulation and presentation of:

- Who you are (professionally; a likable and trustworthy influencer, expert, thought leader, or authority)

- What you offer (and why it's unique to you)

- How this connects (with what people want)

Based on these, here are 10 things that are critical for you to keep making people aware of:

1. Your unique perspective/framework/approach

2. How well you synthesize and deliver information so it's manageable, accessible, understandable, and offers a new insight or twist

3. How consistent you are in your communications (for top-of-mind awareness)

4. How many places you can be found in the marketplace

5. How many raving fans you have (not just browsers)

6. How current your brand feels

7. What level of clientele you work with (based on your level of expertise at the current time, while holding the intention to take it to the next level)

8. How long you have been serving

9. Your energy and passion (as others experience it)

10. The stories you tell about yourself and other people.

By integrating these 10 components into your regular communication—you'll automatically be positioned as the person who has the answer or solution that your clients, customers, colleagues or audience are looking for—or the message, product, or service that will help them discover the answers and solutions.

Think of it like this, by considering these two images:

1. **You're standing in the river.**

If you want to catch more fish, you'll be more successful if you're standing in the river with a net than if you're standing on the shore and yelling, "Hey, fish, come over here; I have what you want!"

- Said another way, it's almost impossible to influence people to click, follow, read, buy, or invest in what you offer if you position yourself in and around something that nobody wants or they're not looking for (even if you know they need it).

2. **You're standing in the river, away from the crowd.**

While you want to be where the fish are, you don't want to stand in the part of the river where everyone else is fishing because it's too crowded.

- Said another way, the goal of your positioning is to express who you are—through your business—in a unique way, so you can stand out in the marketplace or in your niche. Then, people will be attracted to you because they need what you offer, and they realize you're the right person (or company) to serve them.

EXAMPLE. When I launched my businesses and wrote my books (*Marketing With A Heart* and then *Influence With A Heart*), I recognized the need for quality leadership, influential communication, and ethical marketing.

To begin, I recognized that people in every industry are always looking for expert, trustworthy help who delivers real outcomes. (I'm standing in the river.)

At the same time, I was able to differentiate myself and create success by adding the "With a Heart" component. (I'm standing in the river, away from the crowd.)

Because, these days, most people don't want:

- Old-school, sleazy "used-car-salesman" marketing
- Communication that lacks empathy and connection
- Command-and-control leadership

They want leadership, communication, and influence that's ethical, delivers exceptional value, and aligns with their principles of integrity, trust, value, and service.

That's why people kept hiring me for speaking, coaching, and consulting. It gave me more reach, I got a better response, and, therefore, I was able to produce more results (for my clients and myself). And I'm happy and grateful to report that this keeps happening.

One of the Biggest Mistakes Thought Leaders Make When Communicating

My friend Jorge is a dynamic and dynamite speaker and leader.

The first time I saw him, I was riveted. He delivered the perfect combination of information, inspiration, and stories that made his teaching come alive and influenced a powerful perspective shift in his audience.

But when I saw how he wrote—uh oh.

Have you ever noticed how some smart, influential people don't always write the way they speak?

That's Jorge.

When he speaks to an audience—or one-on-one—he's flawless.

His written words, however, are kind of flawed.

And this is a big problem because people aren't subscribing to his email list. (Jorge wants to build his list so he can attract more business and not rely solely on speaking gigs, networking, and referrals.)

He and I spent some time looking at his website, emails, blog posts, and the language (and incentive) he's using to invite people to join his list.

I analyzed what he wrote with an understanding of what he was trying to accomplish.

His 7 biggest mistakes (which are common for many consultants, influencers, experts, authors, and thought leaders) were these:

1. Too many words and too many big words

2. Too many ideas at once that were too complex and abstract

3. Too many tangents, sidebars, and open loops

4. Too many long sentences with too many commas

5. Too little focus on what the client (or customer or audience) really needs (not what he thought they needed)

6. Too little focus on this person's (or group's) fears, frustrations, challenges, aspirations, goals, or dreams—described from their perspective and experience—in their language

7. Too little focus on "connecting the dots." What kind of transformation are you offering? Why is this so important in this person's business or life? Why are you uniquely suited to serve this person—or these people—more than anyone else out there?

The results of these mistakes?

1. Fewer people read. Not so many take action. Hardly anyone invests.

2. Less reach, response, and results (lots of wasted time, money, and energy). Less impact.

I offered a solution that Jorge was able to implement right away: record what you say into dictation software that automatically transcribes (like Otter.ai).

Here's why it works:

Just like Jorge, when you create any kind of content—whether it's an email, blog post, training, speech, video, book, Facebook post, webinar, information product, or basically anything—you'll want to communicate with people in your voice.

Not your academic or business voice. YOUR VOICE.

The voice that speaks your truth and shows people that you can help them overcome their challenges and reach their goals and dreams.

Since the words from Jorge's mouth are clearly hitting their mark, all he needs to do is get them down on paper, so to speak.

Then he can use his own words (the ones that are inspiring and influential) to write his emails, update his website, refine his LinkedIn summary, and make his opt-in content better and more valuable.

Here's how Jorge did it—and how you can do it, too:

Create an outline (as you would for a speech, presentation, article, blog post, webinar, or training) that describes these four things:

1. Who you are, what you do, and why you're uniquely suited to do it like nobody else on the planet.

2. The transformation you help people create—at home, at work, or in their lives—and connect this to your story.

(You'll be extra influential if you share how you discovered your knowledge and earned your wisdom.)

3. The 1-3-5 steps/ways/methods a person can begin that transformation, starting today.

4. The best next action for this person to take.

Then talk your way through the outline in your own voice (whether you're dictating or getting it transcribed).

Because, when you communicate with people in your voice, you're able to accomplish four things:

1. You connect deeply, clearly, and on an emotional (as well as expert) level, whether it's with your prospects, customers, clients, colleagues, or anyone who is important for your business)

2. You create rapport, so you can give people the opportunity to know you, like you, trust you, and see that you are a credible authority or leader

3. You deliver valuable information, that makes a powerful transformation in their business or their life

4. You invite them to take action, that's good for them and good for you

That being said, are you ready to record?

7 Reasons Why the Buddha Was (and Still Is) an Influential Thought Leader

For more than forty years, the Buddha served people by teaching a nonsectarian (non-religious) way to live a more harmonious life where happiness comes from the inside and doesn't depend on what's happening outside of us.

He discovered a practice that worked for him, worked for other people, and could be taught.

His message, teaching, and how he delivered them have created an ongoing legacy and made him one of the most influential thought leaders in human history.

Here are 7 reasons why:

1. The Buddha taught that each of us has an opportunity to change what we think, say, and do, so we can live happier, more peaceful, and more successful lives.

2. He tailored his vision, message, and teaching to his audience. He spoke to people in their language. He met them where they were, not where they "should" have been.

3. The Buddha used story to provide a holistic, memorable learning experience. His teachings were accessible, applicable in daily life, and gave immediate and long-term benefits.

4. He always invited people to verify the results for themselves and not just accept them on blind faith.

5. The Buddha presented his teachings simply and directly as frameworks, steps, and a clear process. He made sure that his teaching was available to everyone who wanted to listen and practice.

6. To keep the teachings intact and available for generations to come, he always followed the same core, guiding principles.

7. The Buddha aligned his mission, vision, principles, and message.

These became his 'brand' and inspired evangelists who shared his message for the subsequent 2,600 years (and counting)!

That's why the Buddha was (and still is) an influential thought leader.

[What Are Your Thoughts or Insights?]

Case Study: Pivoting, Positioning, and Profiting

OPPORTUNITY A boutique tech company wanted to attract more businesses with positive social impact. The founder also wanted more time to volunteer, by teaching.

BACKGROUND The company was known for an app that helps California wine growers reduce water usage and costs. They created technology for a healthcare system to improve services for people with AIDS (50 states).

SOLUTION I guided the founder in identifying and clarifying the new positioning which created two client pipelines: 1) leaders/decision makers; and 2) developers. Although two different markets, they wanted the same outcomes. They just spoke about them differently. As a result, we adapted the marketing and communications to effectively accommodate these insights while presenting the founder as a thought leader.

We transformed his entire website, LinkedIn summary and tagline, social media, elevator pitch, opt-in content, email sequence, discovery call script, and then we began developing a product.

RESULTS New business is already coming in via both pipelines, and the founder has just been asked to teach at a big tech event in San Francisco.

ACTION: Are You a Thought Leader? (Make Sure People Know These 7 Things About You)

1. Your position, title, job, role, company, etc.

2. Your professional path (your successes, case studies, etc.) as well as your earned wisdom from your "failures")

3. The fact that you do a lot of good for a lot of people already as indicated by your many testimonials

4. Anytime that you appear in the media or press, as seen on, as quoted in, as featured in, etc.

5. Your partnerships and connections to influencers

6. Your philosophy, framework, "special sauce," etc.

7. Your book, awards, testimonials, accolades, products, inventions, innovations, etc.

People's perception of you as a thought leader is key. Make sure people know. Tell them in multiple ways.

Don't worry about repeating yourself. Repetition is your friend, and the right people are ready to listen.

Do You Want to Publish, Position, and Profit from Your Book?

Then you'll want to do it right, do it fast, and do it with a trustworthy team who will help you with every step from manuscript to money to making a bigger impact.

1. Book strategy (from publishing over 10,000 books)

2. Top-notch cover, interior design, and ebook design

3. Spot-on editing and proofreading

4. Handling the other 351 steps of publishing

   (getting you ready for launch: ebook, paperback, hardcover, and all the little details in the mix)

5. A professionally produced and narrated audiobook

6. Your positioning and messaging (so you can stand out in the hearts and minds of the people you serve)

   1. Your LinkedIn summary and tagline
   2. Your 100-word intro for referrals, interviews, podcasts, etc.
   3. Your elevator pitch and expertise framework

4. how to talk the value of your offer (10X) so more people (unhesitatingly) say YES(!) to you

7. Your book done and getting you business. Congratulations!

Ready to get started? Visit PublishPositionAndProfit.com or reach me directly here: ben@influencewithaheart.com

Wrapping It All Up

In those fateful seventy-two hours in India, when I almost died four times, my life flashed before my eyes. Because of that, I'd like to leave you with an important thought:

"When your life flashes before your eyes, make sure it's something you want to watch!"

Because you're amazing and there's nobody like you!

You already impact and transform people's businesses and lives through what you offer.

Are you ready to turn up the volume?

Are you ready to write your book?

The path is simple. It all starts when you communicate with more influence by using more empathy, story, and thought leadership.

- Why? Your clients, customers, colleagues, or audience need to get inspired and excited about who you are and what you offer so they can take action that's good for them and good for you.

- They must understand that you are an authentic influencer, expert, authority, or thought leader who understands and cares about them.

(And then they will tell others about you and how you've impacted their business or life.)

The fastest, simplest way to inspire and influence more people (ethically) is by using more empathy, story, and thought leadership every time you communicate.

(Plus a dash of loving-kindness.)

You can do this anytime, anywhere, with anyone: in person, online, onstage, on the phone, in a training, in a video, during a speech, or in a meeting. Whether you're communicating with 1, 10, or 10,000 people, it works.

Think about all the people who need what you offer, and are waiting for you right now. Imagine the impact that you will make!

Realize that you now have a powerful framework and an array of strategies and approaches to make it happen.

(I promised I would teach you that in this book. And that's what I've shared. Thanks for reading.)

THE CORE TEACHING: When you communicate with more influence, you inspire more people and make an even bigger impact. This means using more empathy, story, and thought leadership (with a dash of loving-kindness).

1. Loving-kindness is the wish and intention for yourself (and all beings) to be happy, safe, peaceful, and free. It happens when you relax your head, relax your face, smile, and feel the love in your heart. Then you share it by smiling at others.

2. Empathy allows you to see the world through another person's eyes and connect with them from a place of authenticity, integrity, and service.

3. Stories reach people's hearts as well as their minds. Your stories create inspiration by creating an emotional experience for your reader or listener.

4. Thought leadership comes from your "special sauce." This is your years of experience, discovery, hard-earned wisdom, education, "failures", triumphs, anecdotes, mishaps, joys, insights, training, investments, wisdom, time, energy, and love.

In conclusion, by using The Influence With A Heart® Method seven wonderful things happen:

1. You'll be positioned as an expert, influencer, authority, or thought leader who people know, like, and trust. (So when people invest in your training, service, product, or program—or get behind you and your vision—they will be even more invested in their success, and therefore your success.)

2. You'll inspire and invite people to change their thoughts so they can choose to change their behaviors and transform their business or their life.

3. You're able to offer unique perspectives, tools, and techniques, so the people you reach can be more successful and make a bigger impact in their world.

4. More people will say yes to your ideas, vision, message, products, and services, whether it's your clients, customers, audience, colleagues, partners, employees, stakeholders, team, or the media.

5. More people will take action because more people will have the opportunity to have their business or life transformed by what you offer.

6. You'll create influence (with a heart) because you'll connect people to each other and build a bridge from your vision to their goals and dreams so everyone will benefit from the gifts and insights that you offer to the world.

7. The people you impact will become your fans, clients, tribe, customers, community, referral network, affiliate partners, and more, bringing a flood of new and repeat business to your door so you can make an even bigger impact!

That's what Influence With A Heart® is all about.

And that's why it's time to write your book.

I want to offer you so much gratitude and respect for doing all of the amazing things you do in this world!

Cheers,

Ben

P.S.

Isn't it time to get your book done? Connect with me today at InfluenceWithAHeart.com/connect

Acknowledgements

As often as I can throughout every single day, I give thanks. I'm so happy and grateful for all the blessings I have and all the blessings I'm receiving.

I'm grateful for everyone and everything that supports my life and makes it possible for me to make my unique impact in the world.

May all beings express themselves fully, act with more compassion, help more people, and live free from suffering.

###

And to everyone who helped in the physical, digital, spiritual, and inspirational production of this book... my family, Joseph Ranseth, Annemarie Schrouder, James Woeber, the Evolutionary Business Council, George Schofield, Linda de Mello, Lou D'Alo, Mag Dimond, Bo Liu...

... Rainbow Xue, Chris O'Byrne, Haisam Hussein, Debbie O'Byrne, Ralph Miller, Alia Shah, Laura Branagan, Zeke Kossover, Goa Gil, Quito & Gozzi, Pico & Nano, Intel (font: Clear Sans), Apple (font: San Francisco), Bhante Vimalaramsi, David Johnson, Ananda, and the Buddha.

Printed in Great Britain
by Amazon